Inventing the American Woman

D1374036

ARTHUR S. LINK
Princeton University
GENERAL EDITOR FOR HISTORY

Inventing the American Woman

A PERSPECTIVE ON WOMEN'S HISTORY 1607–1877

GLENDA RILEY
University of Northern Iowa

HARLAN DAVIDSON, INC.
Arlington Heights, Illinois 60004

Library of Congress Cataloging in Publication Data

Riley, Glenda, 1938–
    Inventing the American woman.

    Bibliography: p.
    Includes index.
    Contents: v. [1] 1607–1877
    1. Women—United States—History. I. Title.
HQ1410.R55   1986   305.4'0973   85-21880
ISBN 0-88295-837-2 (v. 1)

*For the generations
of students and colleagues
who contributed
to my understanding of
and commitment to
the history of women
in the United States*

Contents

Acknowledgments

So many people have contributed to the genesis of this book over the years that it is impossible to name them all. Two historians of women who have been particularly supportive of the project are D'Ann Campbell and Sandra L. Myres. Two of my colleagues who have encouraged the writing of the work and offered help with details are Harold B. Wohl and William H. Graves. One who deserves special mention for his perceptive critiques and insightful suggestions is Richard S. Kirkendall, Henry A. Wallace Professor of Agricultural History at Iowa State University.

The project was supported in part by a professional development leave from the University of Northern Iowa. The staff of the UNI Library contributed greatly to its progress, always with unflagging good humor. Patricia Murphy proved to be an accurate and willing typist. And Karmen Berger served as an energetic and often creative research assistant and "gopher."

The work finally reached completion through the warm and enthusiastic support of the late Harlan Davidson; the press's general editor for history, Arthur S. Link; and its executive editor, Maureen Gilgore Hewitt. The style of the manuscript improved notably through the efforts of Susannah H. Jones.

To all of these people, as well as those who remain unnamed, I am grateful.

Inventing the American Woman

This 1831 illustration entitled The Wife *shows a woman who is expected to do little to occupy herself except sit idly, resting and fanning, as her husband intently reads.* From Godey's Lady's Book, Philadelphia, Pennsylvania.

Prescription and Protest

Y OU may be asking yourself why you have not encountered a number of texts on women's history during your high school and college careers. You may be wondering why the story of American women has seemed to come to light only so recently. Actually, interest in the history of women is not a recent development. Americans of many eras have considered women's experiences worthy of record.

In the early 1830s, for example, *Godey's Lady's Book,* the largest selling periodical of its day, offered its readers historical sketches of women as a regular feature. An early book-length study analyzing women in the American past appeared in 1848. Elizabeth Fries Lummis Ellet, a well-known author, published a two-volume work entitled *The Women of the American Revolution,* which used oral history to recount the contributions of women to the Revolutionary War. In 1854, writer Lydia Maria Child also wrote a two-volume history of women. Entitled *History of the Condition of Women,* it spanned ancient to modern times. In 1898, yet another two-volume work, Sydney Fisher's *Men, Women, and Manners in Colonial Times,* stressed the contributions of women to American agriculture. Many other similar books and articles written by both women and men appeared throughout the nineteenth century.

By the turn of the twentieth century, many historians who had received formal training in the new American graduate schools began to join these lay historians in recording and analyzing the course of historical events. Because they usually concentrated on political and economic events such as wars, depressions, acts of Congress, and presidential policies, groups of people such as women, blacks, American Indians, immigrants, and "common" men were generally overlooked. A group of reform-minded historians known as Progressives, however, soon began to attack this view of history. During the 1920s, Arthur M. Schlesinger, Sr., in particular, raised serious questions about the virtual absence of women in most history textbooks. He called upon historians to expand their outlook to include females as well as males.

Although Schlesinger's words often fell on deaf ears, several historians took his challenge seriously. In 1938, Julia Cherry Spruill wrote a detailed survey of women's lives and labors in the southern colonies. In 1946, Mary Ritter Beard published *Women as Force in History* to demonstrate that women indeed deserved inclusion in the historical record. Beard's thoughtful and well-reasoned study presented an important argument for increased recognition of women's history. A few others followed Beard's lead. During the next few decades, some fine women's history was written yet did not receive widespread attention.

The emergence of the contemporary feminist movement in the 1960s dramatically revised this situation. No longer willing to accept historical "invisibility," feminist leaders called for exposure of women's historical heritage. They demanded that women's lives and experiences receive attention from all types of scholars, and especially from historians. No longer, they warned, would women tolerate being denied a sense of value and identity by near omission from the historical record.

Possessing an increased social consciousness as a result of the various reform crusades of the 1960s, many historians responded enthusiastically to the call to retrieve women's history. They undertook a sincere attempt to remedy the omissions, usually by adding unusual or important women to historical studies and textbooks. But change was slow and difficult to effect. In 1976, I conducted a survey of American history textbooks that revealed a discouraging picture. In a textbook written in 1972, one that offered a 409-page survey of the "complicated story" of "our national history" before 1877, only 5 women appeared as opposed to 278 men. Four of these women were covered in the only three paragraphs on women's history in the entire text. A 478-page work published in 1975 included 13 women and 406 men. Out of almost ninety illustrations, only four pictured women. Here, the topic of women's history was dealt with in less than four pages. These were typical of the large number of American history textbooks examined.

In addition, these volumes concentrated on famous women and those who participated in the woman suffrage movement. Black, American Indian, Mexican-American, and other racial and ethnic groups of women were seldom mentioned. Working, frontier, southern, and other types of women were similarly ignored. Most historians still used the pronouns "he," "him," and "his" as generic terms that subsumed women. And they continued to refer to women condescendingly as "the gentler sex" while characterizing suffragists as "petticoats in revolt" and "a belligerent bevy of female agitators."

Despite these problems, both historians and the public began to realize that women had been given short shrift in history. More encouraging yet was the willingness of many historians to try to correct the situation. A new breed of historians, women's historians, began to emerge in the late 1960s and early 1970s to aid in the development of this "remedial history," as it soon came to be known. At first they concentrated on correcting the traditional omission of women, primarily by writing famous women into historical accounts. They quickly turned their attention to more sophisticated analysis. Both female and male historians of women began to explore questions relating to the oppression of women, their political activities, involvements with home and family, participation in reform movements, and changing roles in different eras. At the same time, they began to call for an integration of women's history into all history courses. They often naively believed that, once they had established the validity of women's history and integrated it into historical knowledge as a whole, their task would be finished.

As the study of women's history progressed and grew throughout the 1970s and 1980s, its complexity and vast scope became increasingly apparent. It also became obvious that women's history could not be dealt with simply by establishing a "compensatory" history that would interject women's contributions into a male-oriented past. The story of women's lives through time was so intricate that it clearly demanded ongoing study by many scholars who would be willing to devote entire careers to its pursuit. Consequently, women's history and the larger field of women's studies became well-established areas of research, study, and instruction. Many specialized journals, such as *Women's Studies, Signs,* and *Women's History,* now exist. The American Historical Association and the Organization of American Historians recognize women's "conference groups" within their organizations, important steps in legitimizing the field of women's history. Since 1973, six Berkshire Conferences on the history of women have been held. Numerous other conferences and scholarly sessions are now held every year. And thousands of women's history and women's studies courses and programs are now offered in American schools, colleges, and universities. Still, experts agree that the surface of the study of women has just been scratched.

Despite this trend toward specialization, historians interested in women are still dedicated to integrating knowledge about them into other history courses. A movement often called "mainstreaming" is currently afoot to encourage instructors and students alike to focus on the history of their collective past rather than on only segments of it. Like the early feminists, proponents of mainstreaming argue that women should not be denied their historical heritage. But they also add that inadequate coverage of women is unfair to men as well because it produces a biased view of the past. Reaching these women and men with a more balanced version of history requires efforts that range beyond specialized courses. Advocates of mainstreaming firmly believe that it is the function of the introductory history course to present students with a comprehensive and inclusive approach to the past.

This book, *Inventing the American Woman*, is an effort to simplify the incorporation of women's history into the basic introductory course on United States history. It recognizes that instructors often do not have the time and energy to conduct thorough research in new materials that they would very much like to offer their students. Thus, it presents an introduction to the history of women in the United States that combines factual knowledge with a specific thesis intended to provoke discussion and further thought. It is my hope that it will inform, enlighten, and expand the thinking of all who read it.

In an attempt to achieve these goals, this book necessarily emphasizes what historian Kathryn Kish Sklar terms "gender specific" experiences. It focuses on those historical episodes that are more germane to one gender than the other. Specifically, women's work, socialization, roles, activities, and cultural values are of primary concern. Due to limitations of time and space, "human specific" occurrences, or those that involve both men and women, often receive little attention. As Sklar argues, it is often necessary to divide and reduce complicated reality in order to analyze its various components. In this case, women's history is separated from human history to make it manageable and understandable.

More specifically, this volume compares the model that was to direct American women's behavior with women's reactions to it. The model was created by generations of both women and men who accepted certain enduring "truths" regarding women. To them a real American woman intrinsically was, among other things, a devoted mother, an unusually virtuous person who had to remain aloof from the corruption of politics, a domestic individual who labored most happily and productively within her own home, and a weak-minded, physically inferior being who needed guidance from stronger and wiser people—men. Once accepted as truths, these ideas were embodied in a series of intricate images and stereotypes that defined and limited women's roles. In other words, people invented the American woman.

All cultures invent roles to achieve certain objectives. A variety of scholars and commentators have offered their ideas concerning the purpose served by the model American woman. Some argue that a narrow, domestic image was the creation of selfish men who conspired to keep power and privilege for themselves. Others suggest that a limited sphere for women assured the continuing consolidation of political power in the hands of an elite, prevented disquieting shifts in the nation's labor force, and forestalled anxiety-producing changes in such areas as the family, education, and social life. Yet others point out that confining women to certain activities was a logical outcome of most earlier periods of world history in which men were usually dominant.

It is not the purpose of this book to endorse any of these views. It does argue that the model was confining, tension-producing, and, at most times, outmoded, despite the fact that generations of American women and men clung tenaciously to it. These people apparently found stereotypes of women helpful or comforting. Perhaps the idealization of women seemed to ensure the continuation of a customary and thus comfortable way of life. In other words, the idea of women's separate sphere was familiar and known, like an old shoe. Never mind that the shoe's broken last and outmoded heel prevented it from functioning properly. A new shoe might create new, unknown problems.

As a result of this kind of thinking, untold numbers of women were compelled to accept the dictates of the invented image and attempted to fulfill its many precepts. If they had misgivings, questions, or doubts as they strove to develop their domesticity and accept their imputed weaknesses, many managed to keep them to themselves. Perhaps at such times they even convinced themselves that they were in grievous error to question societal prescriptions regarding their feminine nature.

Yet in addition to thousands of such seemingly quiet and accepting women, there were thousands throughout America's history who resisted the model. They openly exhibited and fervently discussed the tensions that they felt. Their feelings of conflict resulted from trying to function as unique individuals while fitting themselves, however torturously, into prescribed patterns. Although these women had distinct hopes, desires, and talents, they found it necessary to adapt their lives to the stereotypes. They accepted the idea that they had to emulate the model in order to be "true" American women. Thus, they valiantly grappled with a demand that they live up to stereotypes rather than develop their own talents and desires.

These women were often displeased that molds had been cast for them rather than opportunities offered. Societal expectations determined almost every aspect of their lives and directed most of their actions. These prescriptions caused women's education to be distinct, segregated, and of inferior quality. They forced women's literature to be narrow, often puerile, and limiting to the mind. And they encouraged women's clothing to be impractical, sexually enhancing, and limiting to the body.

The many women who disliked having to cope with such restrictions on their lives seemed to have split personalities. They continually tried both to achieve the prescribed image and to develop their own personalities. It is on this type of woman that this book concentrates. It maintains that their experience represents the lives of American women to a far greater degree than does that of the docile and supposedly happy women who, at least on the surface, shaped themselves into a facsimile of the accepted model.

The primary object here is to examine from a historical perspective the lives and activities of women who lived uneasily with the invented American woman. Black, American Indian, and Oriental women, for whom the model American woman was a meaningless construct, are also considered. This book deals, as all women's history must, with both the image of the ways women should act and with the manner in which women actually did think and feel. Rather than accepting conventional and largely unfounded descriptions of women's lives, it refers to women's own words and actions as well as to recent analysis by women's history scholars.

The book proceeds through the major eras of early American history by determining the prescriptions for women and examining women's protests against them. It begins with the traditional date of 1607, the year of the first successful English settlement at Jamestown, and concludes in 1877, the year that formally ended the period of reconstruction following the Civil War. This period marked the painful growth, progress, and unification of the American nation. For women, it also brought change, development, and a growing awareness of the benefits of solidarity. The suggested readings at the end of each chapter are designed to lead the interested reader into further study of women's issues and themes for particular periods.

It is hoped that the information offered here will lend insight into the reshaping of the model of American women from simply that of "Adam's rib" to a more dynamic and attractive image.

SUGGESTIONS FOR FURTHER READING

Beard, Mary R. *Women as Force in History.* New York: Collier Books, 1946.
Carroll, Berenice A., ed. *Liberating Women's History: Theoretical and Critical Essays.* Urbana: University of Illinois Press, 1976.
Filene, Peter G. "Integrating Women's History and Regular History." *The History Teacher* 8 (August 1980): 483–492.
DuBois, Ellen. "Politics and Culture in Women's History." *Feminist Studies* 6 (Spring 1980): 28–36.
George, Carol V. R., ed. *"Remember the Ladies": New Perspectives on Women in American History.* Syracuse, NY: Syracuse University Press, 1975.
Gordon, Ann D., Mari Jo Buhle, and Nancy E. Schrom. "Women in American Society: An Historical Contribution." *Radical America* 5 (1971): 3–66.
Gordon, Linda, Elizabeth Pleck, Persis Hunt, Marcia Scott, and Rochelle Ziegler. "A Review of Sexism in American Historical Writing." *Women's Studies* 1 (1972): 133–158.

Hartman, Mary and Lois Banner, eds. *Clio's Consciousness Raised: New Perspectives on the History of Women*. New York: Harper and Row, 1974.

Lerner, Gerda. *The Majority Finds Its Past*. New York: Oxford University Press, 1979.

————. "New Approaches to the Study of Women in American History." *Journal of Social History* 3 (1959): 53–62.

————. "Placing Women in History: Definitions and Challenges." *Feminist Studies* 3 (1975): 5–14.

Moseley, Eva S. "Sources for the 'New Women's History.'" *American Archivist* 43 (Spring 1980): 180–190.

Riley, Glenda. "Is Clio Still Sexist? Women's History in Recent American History Texts." *Teaching History: A Journal of Methods* 1 (Spring 1976): 15–24.

————. "Integrating Women's History into Existing Course Structures." *The History Teacher* 12 (August 1979): 493–499.

Sklar, Kathryn Kish. "American Female Historians in Context, 1770–1930." *Feminist Studies*, 3 (1975): 171–184.

————. "A Conceptual Framework for the Teaching of U.S. Women's History." *The History Teacher* 13 (August 1980): 471–481.

Smith, Bonnie. "The Contribution of Women to Modern Historiography in Great Britain, France, and the United States, 1750–1940." *American Historical Review* 89 (June 1984): 709–732.

Ætatis suæ 21. Aº. 1616.

Matoaks als Rebecka daughter to the mighty Prince
Powhatan Emperour of Attanoughkomouck als Virginia
converted and baptized in the Christian faith, and
Wife to the worll Mr Tho: Rolff.

This portrait of Pocahontas was painted by an unknown English artist after the 1616 engraving of her by Simon van de Passe. It presents her as a Euro-American woman in appearance and dress rather than as an American Indian. Courtesy of the National Portrait Gallery, Smithsonian Institution, Washington, D.C.

CHAPTER I

A Golden Age? Colonial America
1607–1776

THE year was 1607. The English, eager to enter the race for colonies in the new world, had already failed in their attempt to settle the island of Roanoke off the coast of North Carolina. Now they sent a shipload of men to settle in Virginia. Hopeful that they would find rich natural resources similar to those discovered by Spanish colonizers in South America and French colonizers in Canada, these Englishmen looked toward the new land with optimism in their hearts.

Their hopes were soon shattered. After almost destroying themselves in their futile attempts to discover precious metals and other riches, these first English colonists at Jamestown turned to agriculture. They began to grow crops to feed themselves and then tobacco to export to England. It was soon apparent to both them and the mother country that colonization in Virginia would succeed only if it were based on long-term settlement by families that could provide a market for English goods.

This policy depended on the presence of women—a critical factor in English colonization. Not only were their childbearing abilities essential to the success of colonies in North America, but their contributions as laborers, religious and social forces, and wives and mothers were also crucial. Despite the importance of women to the development of early America, however, traditional conceptions of women, transplanted from Europe and surviving the demands of the colonial environment, continued to shape women's lives. Yet the raw new world and the resistance of numerous female colonists modified customary ideas of women's roles and behaviors.

There is evidence that a few women entered the colonial scene in North America very early. Records indicate that a woman named Anne Forest and her maid, Anne Buras, arrived in Virginia in 1608. A few other women probably completed the hazardous journey as well. But the first significant number of women landed in Virginia in 1619 to be sold by their own consent as wives. The London Company of Virginia recognized the need to send women to Virginia if colonial markets and social stability were to develop in the near future. Yet despite their efforts, by the mid-1600s, men in Virginia still outnumbered women by six to one.

In 1620, a group of religious dissenters against the English Anglican Church landed at Plymouth, whose numbers included both males and females. Eighteen women and eleven girls were listed among the passengers of the *Mayflower*. Only four of the women lived until the following spring, while all eleven of the girls survived the first harsh winter. More women followed as a result of their defection from the church and of the Plymouth Company's interest in promoting the increase of families in their colony. But it was not until 1700 that the sex ratio began to equalize in Massachusetts.

As other colonies gradually established themselves, their founders recognized that women constituted an important group of settlers, both economically and socially. Lord Baltimore of Maryland encouraged the immigration of women because he believed that, "when the plantation grows to strength, then it is time to plant with women as well as with men; that the plantation may spread into generations, and not ever be pierced from without." This policy seemed particularly useful for Maryland, which by the 1650s had approximately 600 males and less than 200 females.

The shortage of women in colonial America created an urgent demand for their importation. While some women came to the colonies as wives and daughters, many others came as potential wives. Between 1620 and 1622, Virginia auctioned off 150 "pure and spotless" women for eighty pounds of tobacco. Other women came as kidnap victims of agents who saw potential gain in selling them as wives. And hundreds of others arrived as petty criminals sentenced to deportation by governments eager to decrease the population of their prisons while increasing that of their colonies.

A large number of women came to America as indentured servants. These were single women between the ages of eighteen and twenty-five who sold their labor for four to seven years in return for their passage, support during their indentures, and a small amount of cash and clothing at the end of their terms. It has been estimated that as many as half of female colonists came as indentured servants, going first to the southern colonies, and later to the middle and New England colonies. During the 1600s, approximately one third of colonial families employed an indentured servant, who was considered part of the household. Although these servants were engaged primarily in domestic tasks, they were occasionally employed in field work as well.

Violations of the indenture were punished severely. Both running away and pregnancy merited an extension of service. The latter crime was common since indentured women were not allowed to marry until the end of their terms. In Maryland alone, one fifth of indentured women were charged with "bastardy." A punitive Virginia law passed in 1692, however, indicated that such pregnancies were due to "some dissolute masters" who had "gotten their maids with child." Despite this problem, virtually all female indentures married at the end of their terms, and often married well because of the continuing demand for women.

Despite the pressure to migrate to America, women remained outnumbered by men, often by as much as five or six men to one woman throughout the South. Some historians argue that the relative scarcity of women often gave them some choice of marriage partners as well as a limited degree of independence and power. Although the family was patriarchal in structure, women were valued and protected within it. In 1712, Benjamin Wadsworth, a Puritan minister, stated that a wife, along with the house and rest of the family, "aught to be under the husband's government." On the other hand, colonial husbands were compelled by law to support their wives and to be faithful to them. Both failure to provide and adultery were punishable offenses. Physical punishment of wives was also controlled by law. In 1641, for example, Massachusetts prohibited a husband from abusing his wife "unless it be in his own defense upon her assault." Divorces and separations were also granted to women with grievances.

A good deal of the consideration extended to colonial women derived from their economic contributions, both as domestic artisans in the home and laborers in the barn and sometimes in the fields. Governor William Bradford of Plymouth observed that, when the Pilgrims landed, the women "went willingly into the fields and took their little ones with them to set corn."

Throughout the colonial period ending in the 1770s, women continued to work in the fields during periods of labor shortage. Although they often performed such male-defined tasks, males only infrequently reciprocated by performing women's domestic chores. As a region became more settled, women's work increasingly focused on the house and garden. Their duties in these areas were extensive and often performed under difficult conditions. It was the women's responsibility to translate into usable goods the raw materials generated by the men through planting or hunting. They were the key links in manufacturing raw materials into finished products. In this capacity, they were the equivalent to their families of factories to industrialized societies.

Of all the goods that women produced, food required the most continuous attention. Food production involved processing, preserving, and cooking, all tasks that demanded a great deal of time and expertise. Pickling, preserving, smoking, salting, and drying foods were a few of their many talents in this area. In addition, women manufactured soap from grease and lye, as well as candles from tallow. They cooked and washed over open fires. They milked cows, raised chickens, and tended vegetable gardens.

Women did many other jobs as well. They combed wool and hackled the flax that they spun into thread, wove into cloth, colored with their own homemade dyes, and sewed by hand into clothing. They spent untold hours at their spinning wheels and with their knitting needles. They served as nurses, apothecaries, doctors, and morticians for their families, friends, and neighbors. They were accomplished herbalists who produced a large variety of efficacious medicines. They bore a large number of children during the eighteenth century—the average is thought to have been seven to eight children per woman. Mothers taught their children early school lessons and trained them as laborers. On the "side," these women brought in cash by selling butter, eggs, beeswax, thread, and other goods that they produced. And they assisted in the family business, whether it be farm, plantation, or shop.

This brief description of colonial women's work does not begin to do justice to the breadth and complexity of their duties. Even when New England towns sprang up with shops that sold various kinds of goods, women's work continued to be extremely taxing. And in the South, the romanticized grand dame of the plantation was in reality a hardworking manager, supervisor, hostess, accountant, teacher, and medical practitioner who was responsible for a large plantation community. Thus, despite her locale, the colonial woman was a domestic artisan and economic partner whose labor was a crucial contribution to the settlement and development of the American colonies.

Some scholars argue that it was not only their scarcity but also these economic contributions which gave colonial women a measure of equality with men. Certainly, women and men were comparable in economic function and importance. But the degree of independence that early American women achieved as a result is not easily ascertained. Historian Mary Beth Norton convincingly argues that the colonial years between 1607 and 1776 were not a "Golden Age" for women. She notes that women's economic contributions to the household were not enough to give them a voice in matters deemed to be male prerogatives in a patriarchal system.

Many people of the colonial period firmly believe, however, that women in America had the best possible lives. They often pointed out that colonial women lived in a "Paradise on earth for women" because they could marry if they so desired. George Alsop of Maryland exclaimed: "The women that go over into this province as servants, have the best luck as in any place of the world, for no sooner are they on shore, but they are courted into matrimony, which some of them had they not come to such a market with their virginity, might have kept it until it had been mouldy." Alsop, like most people of that day, assumed that all women desired marriage and would be fulfilled once they entered it.

During the colonial period, marriage was indeed viewed as an ideal life for women. During the seventeenth century, the unbalanced ratio between men and women put pressure on women to marry while yet in their teens. During the eighteenth century, women usually married between the ages of twenty and twenty-three. Throughout this era, nine out of ten women did marry at least once. In his 1692 guidebook for women, entitled *Ornaments for the Daughters of Zion,* Puritan minister Cotton Mather wrote that "for a woman to be praised, is for her to be married."

Single women were often discriminated against because they were considered unproductive. Those women who did not marry were expected to become part of their nearest male relative's household. Here they became unpaid household help. One of their main duties was spinning— thus the term spinster. Single women did, however, enjoy a legal status known as *femes sole.* This meant that they could exercise a few legal rights such as controlling their personal property.

Once married, a colonial woman entered a legal state known as Civil Death or marital unity. This philosophy was derived from English common law and religious tradition. It denied legal existence to a married woman. The tenets of marital unity were summed up in Sir William Blackstone's *Commentaries on the Laws of England in 1765.* By marriage, the husband and wife are one person in law; that is, during the marriage, the very being or legal existence of the woman is suspended or at least incorporated and consolidated into that of the husband, under whose wing, protection, and cover, she performs everything.

In theory, then, a married woman had no legal existence apart from her husband. She could not sign contracts, had no right to her own earnings, was not able to own property, could not vote on civil or religious matters, and automatically lost her children in case of separation or divorce. All of a married couple's property, including their children, belonged to the husband and was controlled by him. This restricted legal status of women was known as *femes covert.* It was based on the widespread belief that women were best represented by their fathers, brothers, or husbands, who had superior knowledge of the world and would speak for the women's best interests.

It should be noted that the legal status of colonial men also changed when they married. Men, who married on the average between the ages of twenty-five and twenty-eight, became legally liable for the support of their wives and children, were responsible for their wives' crimes and debts, and had to leave two thirds of their estates to their families. One story tells of a wife who was fined by the local court for physically abusing her husband; yet he had to pay the fine imposed upon her. In another very different case, that of Hannah Duston of Massachusetts in 1697, her husband collected her reward when she killed ten Indians in a daring escape from captivity.

These provisions were initially easy for women of European, and primarily Christian, background to tolerate; they so closely paralleled the situation to which these women were accustomed. But such strict legal codes soon became awkward in a society in which women were important economically and socially. Women, whose skills were critical to family survival, who could often handle a rifle as well as men, and who effectively ran the family farm or business during men's frequent absences on business, often were not enthusiastic about the legal limitations imposed on them.

Many local courts recognized that men did not in practice always represent women's needs fairly. Consequently, many local courts of equity modified legal codes and laws through their decisions, granting American women a number of rights not enjoyed by English women. Some married women in colonial America could thus own property, enter contracts, and control their own earnings. They could also protect their property through prenuptial agreements if their husbands accepted the provisions. Moreover, widows often took over the family business or trade after their husbands' deaths. During the 1600s and 1700s, widows ran farms and plantations and worked as shopkeepers, merchants, blacksmiths, gunsmiths, and tavernkeepers. As a single woman, or *femes sole,* a widow was allowed to own property, sign contracts, and conduct her own business affairs.

Daily practice also allowed both single and married women more freedom of action than appeared possible in codes of law. Early American women actually exercised a wide variety of rights and were engaged in a large number of nondomestic activities and enterprises. They also ran away from fathers or husbands whom they found abusive or overly restrictive. Colonial newspapers carried many advertisements for runaway women, and church records included many orders for their return. Because of the labor shortage, women could easily find employment in other towns, where they were guaranteed anonymity by the rudimentary communication system of the time. Few seem to have responded to either the advertisements in the newspapers or the church orders by returning to their fathers or husbands.

In addition, women achieved a modicum of independence through employment. In the labor-scarce economy, many women could work at other jobs besides their domestic duties. Research shows that women labored as butchers, gunsmiths, jailkeepers, journalists, midwives, millers, nurses, printers, proprietors and managers of taverns and boarding-houses, shipbuilders, silversmiths, tanners, teachers, and upholsterers. Margaret Philipse of New York became a merchant and shipper of furs in the 1660s. Betsy Ross was an upholsterer in Philadelphia who employed several young men at the time that she is supposed to have designed the American flag.

Women such as Ross often learned their trades through apprenticeships. Like young men, they served apprenticeships with local craftspersons or tradespersons. A young colonial woman would be apprenticed at the ages of eleven to thirteen for a term of service as much as ten years in length. They were cared for, trained in such domestic tasks as spinning and sewing, and were taught to read and sometimes to write. In other cases, women learned their skills through their fathers, brothers, or husbands who practiced a trade in or near the family home. These men frequently sought the aid of the women of the family, who then acquired proficiency through the process of helping. Other trades and professions, such as the practice of midwifery, were passed down from woman to woman. There were thus many means by which a colonial woman could expand her competency beyond the domestic realm.

Many types of source materials offer evidence that a large number of women actually pursued the trades and professions. Records from King Philip's War (1675–1676) indicate that a Mrs. Allen served as an army physician. Some years later, another woman doctor advertised in a New England newspaper that she "follows the midwife and doctress business; cures burns, salt rheum, canker, scald-head, fever sores, rheumatism, and the piles."

The existence of female merchants is demonstrated by another type of advertisement. Registering the protest of several women merchants against local taxes, this advertisement appeared in a New York newspaper in 1733: "We, widows of this city, have had a meeting as our case is something deplorable. We are house keepers, pay our taxes, carry on trade and most of us are she-merchants, and as we in some measure contribute to the support of the government, we ought to be entitled to some of the sweets of it."

Business records indicate that women were involved in a variety of commercial enterprises. For instance, Quaker women on Nantucket Island developed into shrewd traders. With their husbands away a good deal of the time on whaling or trading voyages, they not only ran their family farms but also began to sell dry goods produced from their own flax and wool to the many trade ships passing through the area. Next, they began a profitable enterprise to provision those ships. A French visitor to Nantucket in the 1770s wrote that "the men at their return, weary with the fatigues of the sea, full of confidence and love, cheerfully give their consent to every transaction that has happened during their absence, and all is joy and peace." When the British blockaded the coastline during the Revolutionary War (1776–1783), the women of Nantucket reportedly ran the blockade in order to continue their trade, now at inflated wartime prices.

Land records show that women also exercised property rights that legal codes declared they did not possess. In 1643, Deborah Moody of Long Island received a colonial land grant. Cornelia Schuyler, also of New Netherland, later acquired a holding of 1,300 acres. In the South, Elizabeth Digges possessed a large plantation, 108 slaves, and a lavishly furnished mansion. And in the colony of Maryland, Margaret Brent owned over 1,000 acres of land. Brent was such a powerful and esteemed landholder that she was appointed the executor of Governor Leonard Calvert's will after his death in 1647. Although she thought that her request for two votes in the colonial legislature—one for herself as a freeholder and one as the governor's representative—was justified, the legislators denied it.

These cases of working, professional, and entrepreneurial women are not consistent with the customary image of docile colonial women in their prim white caps and serviceable dresses quietly caring for their homes and families. Yet many colonial writers and speakers exerted a good deal of energy promoting this image of the passive and domestic woman. In the 1660s, Cotton Mather wrote at great length about the domestic talents that a woman should acquire to "enable her to do the man whom she may hereafter have, good and not Evil, all the days of her life." He added that women were more godly and religious than men. "Truly, though a woman may not speak in the church," he observed, "yet she may humbly repeat unto her husband at home what the minister spoke in the church that may be pertinent unto his condition." Clearly, in his view, woman was the spiritual caretaker of her husband. He explained that this was the case partly because "most women have more time to employ in the more immediate service of their souls than the other sex is the owner of." He also emphasized that "the curse in difficulties both of subjection and child-bearing, which the female sex is doomed into, has been turned into a blessing," for "God sanctifies the chains, the pains, the deaths."

Although Mather and others supported a model for women that emphasized virtue, passivity, domesticity, religiousness, and other similar charcteristics, evidence suggests that many colonial women did not take this advice totally to heart. Mather's own secret diary is purported to include a passage explaining his tortured inner struggle over how to respond to the sexual advances of a woman who approached him in his study late one night. Another diary, that of William Byrd, a southern planter, also contradicted the customary image of colonial women. In describing a woman whom he greatly admired, Byrd wrote that she was "a very civil woman who showed nothing of ruggedness or immodesty in her carriage, yet she will carry a gun in the woods and kill deer, turkeys, and shoot down wild cattle, catch and tye hogs, and perform the most manful exercises as well as most men in these parts."

A recent study of women in colonial North Carolina also brings to light some interesting aspects of female behavior that clash with the image. Court and church records indicate many unexpected deeds. Two young women were called into court for swimming nude with two young men in the Chowan River. The most common crime to appear in the records was fornication, or engaging in sexual relations before marriage. Runaway women and illegitimate children were not unusual. Single women often chose their own mates and did not hesitate to elope when thwarted by their parents. Premarital contracts were frequently employed to protect women's property. Once wed, dissatisfied women sought sexual alliances outside of marriage. And when widowed, many women chose to remain single rather than to remarry. These are hardly the lovely southern belles who are customarily portrayed in their hoop skirts gracing the lawns of stately colonial homes.

Clearly, evidence indicates that there was a discrepancy between the model established for colonial women and the reality that many of them achieved. It might even be argued that the ideal was preached so frequently and forcefully precisely because many women fell short of its standards. After all, guides to behavior are not necessary when everyone in the social group understands the rules and abides by them. Perhaps colonial women understood, and even approved of, the rules but did not always find them easy to follow.

Several examples of well-known women suggest that this was indeed the case. Although they sought to become ideal women, factors in their own lives and characteristics of their own personalities led them in other directions. The colonial poet, Anne Bradstreet, is an outstanding illustration of the conflict between the image and the personal reality with which many women grappled. After immigrating to Massachusetts Bay with her husband, Simon, in 1630, she pursued her household duties, bore eight children, and demonstrated her talent as a poet and writer.

Bradstreet was not unaware of women's accepted roles and duties. There were many sermons, statements, and books that clearly spelled them out. Two books published in 1620, *A Good Wife, God's Gift* and *Marriage Duties,* were only a few of the many guidebooks available. And if women deviated from the accepted rules, they were quickly held up to public scorn. The venerable and respected governor of the Massachusetts Bay Colony, John Winthrop, declared in 1645 that Anne Hopkins, the wife of the governor of Connecticut, had "fallen into a sad infirmity, the loss of her understanding and reason, by occasion of her giving herself wholly to reading and writing many books." He explained that "if she had attended her household affairs, and such things as belong to women, and not gone out of her way and calling to meddle in such things as are proper for men, whose minds are stronger, she had kept her wits, and might have improved them usefully and honorably in the place God had set for her."

Yet Bradstreet felt compelled to go on with her writing, often after a long day's work during which she attempted to be the ideal wife and mother. In 1642, she expressed her bitterness regarding the censure that her work drew. "I am obnoxious to each carping tongue," she wrote, "who says my hand a needle better fits." She concluded: "If what I do prove well, it won't advance/ they'll say its stolen, or else it was by chance."

In 1650, a book of her poems, *The Tenth Muse Lately Sprung Up in America,* appeared anonymously in London. Bradstreet was soon identified as its author. Her brother minced no words when offering his opinion of her activities. "Your printing of a book, beyond the custom of your sex, doth rankly smell," he stated in a public letter to her published in London. Despite her discouragement over this episode and her increasing acceptance of the idea that "men can do best, and women know it well," she continued to write.

Six years after Bradstreet's death in 1672, her works were published under the title *Several Poems Compiled by a Gentlewoman in New England.* Present-day poet Adrienne Rich has eulogized her appropriately: "To have written these, the first good poems in America, while rearing eight children, lying frequently sick, keeping house at the edge of wilderness, was to have managed a poet's range and extension within confines as severe as any American poet has confronted."

Bradstreet was not the only New England woman to defy these limitations. The well-known religious dissident, Anne Hutchinson, also contributed jarring notes to the ongoing debate regarding the nature of women. Like Bradstreet, she was cognizant of the type of behavior that the model prescribed for women. Hutchinson, a Biblical scholar, was also fully conversant with the admonition of St. Paul that women should "keep silent in the churches." Yet after her arrival in Boston with her husband, William, in 1634, she increasingly became the center of a religious controversy.

Hutchinson believed that individuals could communicate with the spirit of Christ and interpret Biblical teachings and sermons on their own. Such beliefs were problematic because they threatened the power of the authoritarian Puritan ministers in Massachusetts. Her ideas were termed antinomian, meaning antiauthority. Her beliefs were a social problem as well as a religious one because they provided a way for women to express their frustrations with their limited roles. Antinomians stressed the individual's ability to feel God's grace within, a tenet that minimized the guidance and teachings of ministers. This encouraged women to think and question rather than simply to accept ministerial pronouncements.

Governor Winthrop, fearing the disruption she was causing, denounced Hutchinson as a woman of "a nimble wit and active spirit, and a very voluble tongue, more bold than a man, though in understanding and judgement, inferior to many women." But she would not be quieted and, in direct opposition to the Pauline doctrine of silence, defended her beliefs both in the community and in church. Her charisma and teachings attracted many followers, both women and men. Prominent and affluent merchants and craftspeople who felt constrained in their businesses by church rules supported her. Her views also appealed to a number of women who seemed to be restive and looking for a way to express themselves. Yet Hutchinson was not just a rebel and an agitator. She was also exemplary in fulfilling her prescribed obligations as a woman. She was a devoted wife, the loving mother of fifteen children, and a beloved midwife and nurse.

Despite Hutchinson's stature and the wide respect accorded her, church authorities were upset by her ideas and the growing factionalism in the community that such ideas encouraged. Charging her with both religious heresy and behavior unfitting a female, they repeatedly called her to trial in 1637 and 1638. Here she was told: "You have rather been a husband than a wife, and a preacher than a hearer, and a Magistrate than a subject." Clearly, Hutchinson had stepped out of her "place" and had challenged home, church, and state. Consequently, Hutchinson was banished from the colony and excommunicated from the church. Along with many of her followers, she left Massachusetts Bay, settled in Rhode Island, where she continued her resistance, and then moved to New York. In 1643, Hutchinson, two of her sons, and three of her daughters were killed by American Indians because of a tragic misunderstanding over payment for the land Hutchinson occupied.

Neither Hutchinson's punishment nor her death marked the end of the antinomian controversy or of women's resistance to restrictions on their lives. In 1638, the Massachusetts court ordered a number of other women dissenters to be whipped or cast out of the church. In 1641, Ann Hibbens was excommunicated for slander and was denounced for resisting the authority of her husband, "whom she should have obeyed and unto whom God put her in subjection." In 1644, Ann Eaton, an opponent of infant baptism, was excommunicated for lying and for stubbornness. Twenty-two years after the Hutchinson affair, one of Hutchinson's major supporters, Mary Dyer, was hanged in Boston. As a Quaker proselytizer, Dyer was thought to be "troublesome" and "notoriously infected with error."

A similar problem erupted with the women of Salem, Massachusetts.

Here, women who questioned religious and other authorities were branded witches. Throughout the witchcraft trials of the 1650s and 1660s, Salem tribunals ordered women to be whipped, chained to posts, jailed, excommunicated, and executed. In 1648, for instance, Margaret James was executed for having a "malignant" touch, using suspicious medicines, and acting in an intemperate fashion at her trial.

In a later outbreak of the witchcraft scare during the 1690s, women and a few men were branded witches in some forty other towns, mainly in New England. These women were usually middle-aged, reputed to be contentious, and involved in community affairs. Their accusers were usually young, unmarried women, and children who were perhaps revolting against authority. Indeed, when Massachusetts looked back on the affair in the early 1700s and exonerated all those accused of witchcraft, the legislature contended that "evil spirits" had motivated the accusers, rather than the accused.

Recent work on seventeenth-century witchcraft in New England suggests that women who achieved even a modicum of economic success were more likely to be accused of practicing witchcraft than those who had not. Wives or widows who were active in commerce or participated in business endeavors received an unusually high number of charges and convictions. Whether they were actually religious dissenters or were threats to prevailing conceptions of womanhood is unclear in most cases. But it is evident that their economic activities diverged sharply from Calvinist teachings regarding women.

Women who rebelled against the model of womanhood by becoming business people appeared not only in New England but in the middle and southern colonies as well. In the South, for example, young Eliza Lucas practiced her own brand of noncompliance. Her father served as a governor of Antigua in the West Indies, although her invalid mother was incapable of running the family plantations in South Carolina. In 1739, seventeen-year-old Eliza took over the management of three plantations in the Charleston area. She taught herself bookkeeping, accounting, and other skills needed to run such an extensive business. She also learned all that she could about the cultivation of rice, South Carolina's major crop at the time. She wrote a friend: "I have the business of three plantations to transact, which requires much writing and more business and fatigue of other sorts than you can imagine."

At her father's urging, Lucas began to experiment with other crops. One of these was the indigo plant, which produced a blue dye very much in demand by the British textile industry. Although neighboring planters thought her to be an eccentric young woman, she believed that indigo might pull the economy of South Carolina out of the doldrums.

The path was not easy for Eliza Lucas. She worked in the fields alongside her overseer, studied the involved process of retting the indigo plant into dye-cakes, and finally accepted the aid of a knowledgeable indigo maker sent by her father from the West Indies. This man feared that her success would undermine his own island's sale of indigo. He quarreled with Lucas and sabotaged the retting equipment. Despite these difficulties, Lucas finally produced the plantation's first batch of dye-cakes in 1744. Upon observing her success, neighboring planters sought her aid. She graciously gave them both indigo seeds and advice. Eventually, indigo became the second largest crop for export in South Carolina.

Although she was atypical in many ways, Lucas also embodied the well-bred southern woman. She studied Plutarch, Virgil, French, and shorthand. She was involved in the prescribed female activities of teaching the plantation children, doing needlework, and playing the pianoforte. She kept a letterbook filled with charming phrases and interesting observations that is one of the most significant collections in existence kept by a colonial lady.

In 1744, Lucas married Charles Pinckney, widower of her best friend and twenty years her senior. During their happy marriage, she continued to supervise the family lands while her husband and two of her sons, Charles Cotesworth and Thomas, engaged in politics. She also established the culture of silkworms in Charleston and founded a smallpox hospital. When she died in 1793, George Washington requested the privilege of being one of her pallbearers.

What conclusions can be drawn from the lives of Bradstreet, Hutchinson, Lucas, and the many other women like them? It appears that they personified a resentment and tension that was perhaps experienced by many women when urged to accept roles that did not fit their own talents, interests, and values. Because such women seldom directly articulated or examined their frustrations, it is impossible to assess how clearly they understood their own actions. They did not declare themselves to be supporters of women's rights or feminism. They did not express their ideas in terms of an ideology or a reform crusade for women. Whether they actively chose to resist the model or were simply following their own convictions is thus indiscernible. The fact remains, however, that these women's individual actions did indeed constitute an assault on the accepted image of womanhood.

The contradictions in these women's lives indicate that the history of white women between 1607 and 1776 is complex and does not easily lend itself to generalization. Yet although women's experiences obviously differed from woman to woman, region to region, and decade to decade, an overview can be constructed. There were similarities in the lives of colonial women, whether they lived in the South of the 1660s or in the New England of the 1700s.

Whether she was married or single, the central focus of a white colonial woman's life was her household and family. A typical colonial household might include a married couple, their children, and perhaps an unmarried aunt, uncle, or grandparent. Perhaps as many as one third of these households also included an indentured servant, hired field-workers, or a number of black slaves.

Since the majority of widows chose not to remarry, a large number of households were headed by women. According to a guidebook published in 1750, *A Wedding Ring Fit for the Finger,* this was perfectly acceptable. Its author explained that, "when the great light goes down, the lesser light gets up." In other words, although a wife was subject to her husband when he was present, she could "be sovereign in her husband's absence." The colonial family was based on a patriarchal system in which the husband, if alive, was the recognized head.

In this structure, work was divided according to sex, with women dominating the home and men dominating the fields or other place of business. But the family organization was not to be a dictatorship. Rather, marriage was often referred to as being egalitarian. A wedding sermon in Boston in 1750 stated: "Our ribs [women] were not ordained to be our rulers. They are not made of the head to claim superiority, but out of the side to be content with equality." Particularly in New England, husbands were cautioned by the courts and community opinion to extend honor and respect to their wives. It was also widely assumed that, since men possessed a highly loving nature, their affection for their spouses would soften the hierarchical organization of the family. Thus, Adam's Rib often had a degree of functional equality although her husband directed family affairs.

In spite of the usual image of our foremothers and fathers, sexual intimacy was an important part of their lives. Men, especially among the Puritans, were expected to satisfy the sexual needs of their wives. Failing to do so, whether through impotence or neglect, was cause for divorce. While believing in sensuality within the bounds of marriage, most colonists were strongly opposed to adultery. Such "inconstancy" was punishable by fines, whipping, the pillory, or even death. Legislation in Massachusetts Bay prescribed whipping and the wearing of the "capital letters A.D. cut out in cloth and sewed on their uppermost garments."

Other causes of divorce included desertion, neglect, cruelty, and bigamy. Divorces were easier to obtain in the colonies than in England but were still costly and time-consuming. Since only those with the necessary resources could pursue a divorce, it is assumed that a large amount of informal separation and desertion took place. Unfortunately, people seldom leave written evidence of such actions.

Solid evidence that sexual crimes occurred between women and men exists. A considerable number of children were born as a result of seduction or rape. These occurrences were not always unpleasant or violent. A Virginia woman of the seventeenth century was so pleased with the outcome of her seduction of a man in an open field that she swore to give him "as much cloth as would make him a sheet." But in many cases, women were victims of physically aggressive males. One Massachusetts woman of the same era reported that a man flung her down in the street; another, that her master caught her by the wrist and "pulled her against the side of the bed."

Because sexuality and childbearing played a prominent role in the lives of colonists, women by necessity devoted a large amount of time to pregnancy and childbirth. As has been said, colonial women bore an average of eight children. Wed in 1685, Sarah Steins Place, a typical New England woman, bore her first child in 1686 and her eighth in 1706. These frequent pregnancies were likely to take a mother's life in one out of every thirty cases. Those women who survived would spend almost twenty years with an infant at her side and almost forty rearing her children to adulthood.

Until the mid-1700s, virtually all babies were delivered by female midwives. The term midwife came from the English "mid-wif," or with-women, thus indicating that birthing was exclusively a female affair during these years. Midwives usually held a respected position in the community and were revered as friends as well as medical practitioners. The midwife's primary function consisted of assisting the mother to deliver naturally. She might use herbal teas, wine, or liquor to lessen the pain, but she avoided mechanical devices and drugs. This situation would change drastically with the introduction of formal medical training, licensing, and obstetrical forceps, all of which led to the introduction of male physicians into the delivery room.

Throughout the colonial period, women prepared for childbirth by abandoning corset stays, wearing flat shoes, and refraining from carriage rides. A pregnant woman also avoided "sudden frights, strong passions, or ungratified longings" to protect her unborn child. Guidebooks advised expectant mothers to pray and to contemplate the possibility of death. Anne Bradstreet expressed her own fears of yet another birth in a poem written for her husband in the mid-1600s. "How soon, my Dear, death may my steps attend/ How soon it may be thy lot to lose thy friend."

As the day of the birth approached, the mother-to-be was joined by her mother, aunts, sisters, friends, and the midwife. They laid out linen, readied basins and towels, told bawdy jokes to lighten the tension, walked the expectant mother about to relieve the pain, and held her by the arms as she delivered her baby through a low stool with an open seat. They then helped care for the mother and newborn babe while celebrating its birth with a feast. The father was admitted only briefly, and other men were barred from the chamber for several weeks. The overwhelming tone of the event was one of encouragement, support, and warmth.

Friends and family soon dispersed. The new mother was free to return to her regular round of duties and chores. Her household, now somewhat expanded, received her attention once more. She also resumed the numerous other undertakings that engaged women's minds, energies, and talents during these years.

One of these activities was the production of handiwork and craft work. Women's needlework skills resulted in finely stitched samples, bed rugs, coverlets, pillow shams, and other textiles. Women also hooked, embroidered, and appliqued rugs. They watercolored and embroidered pictures, portraits, and mourning pictures, which recorded family deaths. They painted stoneware crocks, worktables, sewing boxes, and dishes. And they stitched a large variety of quilts, many of which chronicled births, deaths, marriages, and other significant family events. Extant examples of women's craftwork include a bed rug created by Phoebe Billings of Massachusetts during the early decades of the 1700s, a crewel-worked bed ensemble designed by Mary Bulman of Maine during the 1740s, and a firboard or overmantel painting by Sibyl May of Connecticut during the 1750s. Such artifacts, combined with written descriptions of early American women's creations, indicate that colonial women adorned their homes with exquisite folk art demonstrating both originality and talent.

But all of colonial women's activities were not geared toward their homes. Early American women also engaged in welfare by caring for widows, orphans, criminals, the disabled, and the poor in a day when social institutions such as hospitals and prisons were few in number. In addition, women participated in church affairs. Although denied full participation and the right to hold office, most women were expected to attend religious services and ceremonies. Only a minority sect, The Society of Friends, or Quakers, extended to colonial women equality, participation in the ministry, and a reprieve from the doctrine of St. Paul that demanded the silence of women in church. Quaker women also participated in Quaker government through "women's meetings" instituted in 1681. In all other religious organizations of the 1600s and most of the 1700s, however, women's roles were strictly circumscribed.

When the religious revival movement known as the Great Awakening erupted in the colonies in the 1730s and 1740s, women flocked to revival meetings in numbers equal to men. Revivalism offered women more opportunity for social interaction and freedom for self-expression than the more traditional and formal religious services had. A proliferation of meetings, ministers, and sects diffused authority and created an opportunity for women to assert themselves. Women helped to judge members for admission, to select ministers, and to organize religious services. During the 1760s, Sarah Osborn of Newport, Rhode Island, spoke to hundreds of people in her home each week on religious matters.

Perhaps women favored revivalism because most other public spheres were essentially closed to them. Education for women was limited to the basics and to female "accomplishments" such as needlework, singing, and playing the pianoforte. In the South, planters' daughters sometimes acquired some education due to the common practice of allowing young women to sit in on sessions given by tutors hired to instruct young men. Political involvement was also limited. Although women had occasionally voted in early town meetings or spoken out in local gatherings, increased settlement brought with it consolidation of political power in male hands. Not only the vote but also officeholding, judgeships, jury service, and public debate were restricted to men. It is little wonder that scores of energetic and talented women found their outlet through folk art, social service, or religion. Even on the edges of society, along the colonial frontier that slowly pushed westward toward the Appalachian Mountains by the mid-1700s, women found that their labor, childbearing abilities, and other important contributions were valued but not rewarded by inclusion in public life.

Historian Julia Spruill pointed out that, on the North Carolina frontier, women worked alongside their men doing the heavy labor involved in clearing forested land for farms, planting crops, constructing homes and barns, and raising stock. Frontierswomen were esteemed for their domestic skills as well as their abilities outside of the home; yet as settlement progressed traditional ideas of women's work and roles soon appeared. Although women on the colonial frontier might wield a certain degree of influence within their families, they were usually expected to play customary, docile roles publicly.

Of course, all of these generalizations regarding colonial women speak only of the historical experiences of the white women who helped to develop the British colonies in North America. They have little relevance to either the native women who inhabited the land long before their white counterparts arrived or to the black women forced to immigrate to America against their wills.

Anthropologists and historians interested in American Indians are actively engaged in remedying this situation by reconstituting the story of America's native women. To do this, they have to overcome centuries of anti-Indian prejudice that has distorted the picture. Source materials often reflect the idea of either a Noble Savage or a barbarous one. In either case, the image is mythical.

The continent of North America had been populated by a large number of native peoples for thousands of years before European explorers and settlers arrived. American Indians had a rich culture, complex economic and religious life, technology, agriculture, social structure, and a fascinating history of their own. In reality, then, American history begins well before 1607. After the English and other settlers began to fan out along the coast of North America, the Indian presence continued to shape and determine many facets of American history. Indians, for example, contributed their energies as laborers, guides, and teachers of farming, hunting, and other skills. Indian women offered their talents as spouses and companions, traders, craftspeople, and agriculturalists. Among many other contributions, maize, or Indian corn, facilitated the survival and expansion of the colonies. Indian culture and arts bestowed beauty and creativity to the infant white civilization. And the Indians' love of liberty and fierce independence helped to shape the colonists' conceptions of freedom.

Yet American history textbooks have customarily emphasized only one Indian woman, Pocahontas. Held up to generations of Americans as a significant historical figure, her story is indeed an interesting one. This native woman, originally named Matoaka, was the daughter of Powhatan, an Indian king in early Virginia. In 1607, she intervened with her father to save the life of Captain John Smith of Jamestown. Evidently, it was Smith who first called her Pocahontas.

During the following years, the young woman performed many acts of kindness for various Jamestown settlers. In 1613, she met John Rolfe, the colonist responsible for introducing the cultivation of tobacco to Jamestown. When she agreed to marry Rolfe, she was instructed in Christianity and baptized Rebecca. After the couple's marriage in 1614, they lived in Jamestown and had one child. In 1616, they went to England, where Rebecca was presented at court and touted as an Indian "princess." In 1617, Rebecca died and was buried in England. She was virtually forgotten until the mid-eighteenth century, when several authors and playwrights seized her romantic story for their work.

Other examples of biased historical reporting are the many accounts of American Indian women written by missionaries, trappers, traders, travelers, and settlers. Since the majority of them regarded native people as primitive savages to be Christianized, exploited, removed, or exterminated, they frequently viewed native society with a jaundiced eye that tended to magnify, and even create, negative aspects of Indian life. Also, these observers were usually European males from a nonnomadic, agricultural background and were not accustomed to a division of labor in which the women did the village work and the men did the hunting, fishing, and fighting. Consequently, they consistently described Indian women in terms of "squaws."

One typical account of native women written by a missionary in the early 1600s characterized Indian women as "poor creatures who endure all the misfortunes and hardships of life." According to him, Indian women were the servants and slaves of Indian men. Such damaging characterizations bequeathed a very unattractive picture of Indian women to generations of Americans. The image of the "squaw" was far removed from that of the Indian princess. As one bit of doggerel put it, the "squaw" was a "beast of burden, slave, chained under female law from puberty to grave." This stereotype of the squaw, just like that of the princess, continues to cloud Americans' views of early American Indian women.

In addition to problems of biased perceptions, difficulties also arise in gathering source materials. American Indian history is usually based on oral tradition and is passed on by word of mouth from person to person within a native group. Furthermore, it is often guarded jealously from outsiders because it is considered to be a personal and valued possession. The many and complex Indian dialects also made accurate communication and understanding difficult. Researchers thus face many hurdles in collecting evidence. Yet without native sources, they cannot fairly reconstruct the rich historical legacy of the hundreds of different native cultures that existed during the colonial period.

Given these obstacles, it is not surprising that an objective view of the lives of American Indian women has not yet emerged. Nor have the biographies of many early native women been written. The few Indian women who are remembered include Mary Brant, a Mohawk woman, who was a consort of Sir William Johnson, Superintendent of Indian Affairs for the Northern Colonies in the late 1700s. There was also Mary Musgrove, a part Creek woman who became an Indian leader in colonial Georgia; Catherine Tekakwitha, a Mohawk convert to Catholicism, whom missionaries idealized to unconverted Indians; and Nancy Ward, a Cherokee leader, who befriended settlers on many occasions. Like Pocahontas, these women are remembered primarily for their usefulness to whites. Their stories give few clues to the lives of most Indian women during these years.

It is known, however, that contact with English settlers changed the lives of native women in the coastal Algonquian language groups that included the Wampanoag and Narragansett in New England and the Powhatan in Chesapeake Bay. By the 1630s, these bands had been ravaged by plague and smallpox epidemics. By the mid-1600s, the 10 percent who survived were dependent upon such English trade goods as weapons and clothing. Food was produced by their women. Among the agricultural Algonquian, women produced about 90 percent of the food supply through farming. In addition, they fished, gathered wild plants, produced domestic household goods, processed and stored food, and aided in hunting.

While many observers felt that native women were overburdened with work, others suggested that their lives were not as demanding as they at first appeared. For instance, Roger Williams, religious leader and founder of Rhode Island, noted that native women and men worked together on such tasks as clearing a field for cultivation or harvesting a crop. Mary Jemison, an Indian captive during the 1700s, reported that women's chores were "not so severe" and "probably not harder" than those performed by white women.

Moreover, native women held power in a number of areas. They routinely acted as businesspeople and entrepreneurs by actively engaging in barter and trade. Among themselves, they exchanged crops and other goods; to the English they offered skins, baskets, and other items in return for needles, textiles, kettles, tea, stockings, and shoes. In addition, women could wield influence by rising to the position of leader, or sachem. Although the office of sachem was inherited, it was retained only by keeping the respect of the group who supported the sachem with contributions of food. Quaiapan served as a Narragansett sachem during the 1660s and 1670s, while Weetamoo led as many as 300 Pocasset Indian men in warfare during those years. Native women also served as shamans, or priests. In this role, they acted as religious leaders and medical practitioners. Among some bands, women even served as both shamans and warleaders, a position that involved much power and respect. Finally, many native groups were matrilineal and matrilocal, patterns that underwrote the influence of women in both their families and bands.

Colonial observers were perhaps misled about the supposedly "degraded" position of native women by the system of sexual segregation observed among most coastal Algonquian groups. Women often ate separately, performed their own dances, and spent their menstrual periods in special huts. At the same time, sexual assault and other vulgar behavior was virtually unknown, with rape being the only capital offense punishable by the entire band. When native women's roles as agriculturalists, domestic laborers, and people of influence were observed by later generations of Euro-Americans among inland and plains Indians, the prism of white culture, values, and belief systems once again distorted the picture.

The history of early black women has fared even worse than that of native women. Since blacks were considered lowly and inferior, their experiences were recorded only incidentally. Records of the London Company show, for instance, that the first load of 20 blacks arrived at Jamestown in 1619. By 1648, Virginia's black slave population had reached 300. Various records indicate that blacks lived and labored not only in the colonial South, but in the middle and New England colonies as well. For example, laws of several northern colonies and of all the plantation colonies demonstrate the strong sentiment that existed against miscegenation, that is, interbreeding of whites and blacks. And diaries and letters of early settlers frequently mention black field hands and women who served as nursemaids, washwomen, and domestic servants.

Blacks, like Indians, were viewed with great prejudice. They, too, were seen as uncivilized barbarians who knew nothing of Christianity. Brought from a far and unknown land in chains, black slaves seemed to most colonists to be sons and daughters of Satan. It is thus understandable that one of the few existing accounts of an early black woman is that of Tituba, a West Indian slave accused of practicing witchcraft in Salem.

As the number of blacks in America increased, so did the fears of the whites. By the close of the colonial period in the 1770s, there were 48,460 black slaves in the North and 411,362 in the South. Whites increasingly viewed blacks as troublemakers who rebelled or ran away. Indeed, both slave men and women often ran away, according to public notices and newspaper advertisements for their return. One such announcement that appeared in the *South Carolina Gazette* in 1834 stated: "Run away about five weeks ago from Hugh Campbell, a Negro wench named Flora, she has a scar on her forehead." Flora's owner offered a thirty shilling reward for her return.

White worries about runaways and rebellions eventually led to the denial of education for and written communication between black people on the theory that such opportunities would only foster conspiracies among slaves. Denied a written outlet for their thoughts and used to the custom of oral history from their African homes, black Americans relied on oral tradition to register their history. Historian Gerda Lerner has pointed out that black women's history faces another predicament. As a group, black women have been the target of double oppression. They have been discriminated against as blacks and as women. This leads to the neglect of their history by both black historians and women's historians. If they appear in history textbooks at all, it is usually often as hapless victims of the slave system.

Actually, the first black women to come to the colonies did so as indentured servants, a temporary status during which the black woman's labor was exploited in both house and field but that was supposed to end after a period of years. As early as the 1640s, however, Virginia court records noted that black people were sold "for life" and that the status of many black children was that of "perpetual servant." In 1652, one Virginia planter purchased a young black woman as well as "her issue and produce during her . . . Life tyme and their successors forever." By 1662, slavery was legalized in all the colonies.

The issue of the legal position of black women was soon resolved. In 1662, Virginia passed legislation decreeing that all black children would automatically inherit their mother's condition, that "all children born in this country shall be held bond or free according to the condition of the mother." It also stated that any "Christian" that was engaged in "fornication with a Negra man or woman, he or she offending shall pay double the fines imposed." Other colonies soon followed suit with laws supporting black slavery and forbidding miscegenation. By the mid-1700s, every colony prohibited cohabitation between the races.

Black women in colonial America were plagued with heavy workloads, broken families, and a short life expectancy created largely by a lack of immunity to unfamiliar diseases. Although black women who produced many children were highly valued, their poor health, early death rates, and depression and alienation under slavery created a low fertility rate. In addition to producing future workers, black women were also expected to provide cheap labor. In the South, the black slave woman was put to work in both plantation house and fields, while in the North she engaged in domestic tasks or was hired out.

Black slave women, much like American Indian women, played a vital role in the colonial economy. Yet their contributions were frequently overlooked and undervalued. Another conclusion that can be drawn regarding native and black women in early America is that their lives, roles, and actions frequently diverged from the Euro-American ideal of womanhood. Rather than being passive and weak, they were often assertive and strong. Although they did cook, sew, and care for their families, they also performed heavy labor, resisted their oppressors, and filled leadership roles. Like many of their white counterparts, the reality of their lives regularly deviated from the myth of what they "should" be.

The process of inventing the model of the American woman had only begun during the years of settlement. The colonial period was not only the childhood of the new nation; it was the infancy of the development of the "true" American woman. Traditional ideas of women's roles came to the American colonies as part of the settlers' cultural baggage. Here they were shaped by the demands of the new and often rugged environment.

Gradually, customary views of women experienced alteration. The reality of many women's lives deviated from the prescribed image. During the years after 1776, however, the invented American woman would tend to grow and codify along with a new nation—the United States of America.

SUGGESTIONS FOR FURTHER READING

Anderson, Marilyn J. "The Best of Two Worlds: The Pocahontas Legend as Treated in Early American Drama." *The Indian Historian* 12 (Summer 1979): 54–59, 64.

Barker-Benfield, G. J. "Anne Hutchinson and the Puritan Attitude Toward Women." *Feminist Studies* 1 (1972): 65–96.

Berkin, Carol Ruth. "Within the Conjurer's Circle: Women in Colonial America." In *The Underside of American History*, 3d ed., edited by Thomas R. Frazier, 79–105. New York: Harcourt, Brace and Jovanavich, 1978.

Berkin, Carol Ruth, and Mary Beth Norton, eds. *Women of America: A History.* Boston: Houghton Mifflin Company, 1979. Parts I and II.

Buel, Joy Day, and Richard Buel, Jr. *The Way of Duty: A Woman and Her Family in Revolutionary America.* New York: W. W. Norton & Co., Inc., 1984.

Demos, John. *A Little Commonwealth: Family Life in Plymouth Colony.* New York: Oxford University Press, 1970.

———. *Entertaining Satan.* New York: Oxford University Press, 1982.

Dewhurst, C. Kurt, Betty MacDowell, and Marshal MacDowell. *Artists in Aprons: Folk Art by American Women.* New York: E. P. Dutton, 1979.

Dye, Nancy Schrom. "History of Childbirth in America." *Signs* 6 (Autumn 1980): 97–108.

Friedman, Jean E., and William G. Shade, eds. *Our America Sisters: Women in American Life and Thought.* Lexington, MA: D. C. Heath and Company, 1982. Part I.

Green, Rayna. "The Pocahontas Perplex: The Image of Indian Women in American Culture." *The Massachusetts Review* 16 (1975): 698–714.

Gregory, Chester W. "Black Women in Pre-Federal America." In *Clio Was a Woman: Studies in the History of American Women,* edited by Mabel E. Deutrich and Virginia C. Purdy, 53–70. Washington, D.C.: Howard University Press, 1980.

Gordon, Michael, ed. *The American Family in Social-Historical Perspective.* New York: St. Martin's Press, 1978.

Hubbell, Jay B. "The Smith-Pocahantas Story in Literature." *The Virginia Magazine of History and Biography* 65 (July 1957): 275–300.

James, Edward T., ed. *Notable American Women, 1607–1950: A Biographical Dictionary.* Cambridge, MA: Belknap Press, 1971.

Jordan, Winthrop D. *White over Black: American Attitudes Toward the Negro, 1550–1812.* Chapel Hill: University of North Carolina Press, 1968.

Kessler-Harris, Alice. *Women Have Always Worked: A Historical Overview.* New York: McGraw-Hill, 1982.

Koehler, Lyle. *The Search for Order: The "Weaker Sex" in 17th Century New England.* Urbana: University of Illinois Press, 1980.

Lindemann, Barbara S. "'To Ravish and Carnally Know': Rape in Eighteenth-Century Massachusetts." *Signs* 10 (Autumn 1984): 63–82.

Medicine, Beatrice. "Bibliography of Native American Women." *The Indian Historian* 8 (1975): 51–53.

Norton, Mary Beth. "The Evolution of White Women's Experience in Early America." *American Historical Review* 89 (June 1984): 593–619.

Ryan, Mary P. *Womanhood in America: From Colonial Times to The Present.* New York: New Viewpoints, 1979. Chapter 1.

Scholten, Catherine M. "On the Importance of the Obstetrick Art: Changing Customs of Childbirth in America, 1760–1825." *William and Mary Quarterly* 34 (July 1977): 426–445.

Smith, Daniel Scott, and Michael S. Hindus. "Premarital Pregnancy in America, 1640–1671: An Overview and Interpretation." *Journal of Interdisciplinary History* 5 (1975): 537–570.

Spruill, Julia Cherry. *Women's Life and Work in the Southern Colonies*. New York: W. W. Norton and Company, 1972.

Ulrich, Laurel Thatcher. *Good Wives: Images and Realities in the Lives of Women in Northern New England, 1650–1750*. New York: Oxford University Press, 1983.

Watson, Alan D. "Women in Colonial North Carolina: Overlooked and Underestimated." *North Carolina Historical Review* 58 (January 1981): 1–22.

Wells, Robert V. "Demographic Change and the Life Cycle of American Families." *The Journal of Interdisciplinary History* 2 (Autumn 1971): 273–282.

Woloch, Nancy. *Women and the American Experience*. New York: Alfred A. Knopf, 1984. Chapters 1–2.

Wertz, Richard W., and Dorothy C. Wertz. *Lying-In: A History of Childbirth in America*. New York: Free Press, 1977.

Young, Philip. "The Mother of Us All: Pocahontas Reconsidered." *Kenyon Review* 24 (Summer 1962): 391–415.

This *Charles Willson Peale* portrait of *Mary Gibson Tilghman and her sons was painted in 1789. Done only a year before her death in 1790 at age twenty-four, it might have been a model for the image of the Republican Mother that developed during the Revolutionary era.* Courtesy of the Maryland Historical Society, Baltimore, Maryland.

CHAPTER 2

Republican Motherhood:
The American Revolution and Early New Nation
1776–1816

O N 2 July 1776, the Continental Congress voted to support independence of the American colonies from their mother country. When Congress released the news of independence on July 4, it was the occasion of celebration for those who were Patriots, or supporters of the new government. These people favored a revolution that would lead to the establishment of an independent nation. For Loyalists, those who backed the English, it was the cause of great consternation. These people preferred to remain within the British Empire. But few colonists, whatever their political sympathies, were surprised. A widespread desire for self-government had been evolving for many years due to the economic, social and political differences between Great Britain and her colonies in North America.

Although historians have generally focused on male activities during the American Revolution and when the new American nation was hammered out, women were also highly involved. Despite the fact that women contributed their skills and energies to the growth and progress of their country, they were not rewarded with widely expanded roles and statuses. Instead, the traditional conception of women as wives and mothers survived the Revolutionary era and was in some ways strengthened during these years. Rather than being destroyed by the national upheaval, this conception was increasingly cast in a conventional mold. The idea of women's "sphere" grew in stature and impact. At the same time, in practice, serious questions were being raised concerning its validity in light of women's participation in resistance, war, and the founding of the new nation.

The resistance phase of the colonies can be traced back to 1763, the year in which the French and Indian War ended. Dissatisfied colonists registered unending complaints concerning the provisions of the treaty that concluded the war and the many pieces of legislation that flowed out of Parliament in an attempt to control its unruly American subjects. The usual historical account of the resistance period is marked by such names as Sam Adams, Thomas Hutchinson, Thomas Jefferson, and Thomas Paine, and such organizations as the Stamp Act Congress, the Sons of Liberty, and the Continental Congress.

A major omission from the history of the resistance years are the many contributions of female Patriots. A large number of colonial women involved themselves in resistance to the British almost immediately. They willingly boycotted the importation of many of their favorite goods, especially tea. They formed themselves into anti-tea leagues, in which they experimented with brewing herb teas from raspberry, sage, and birch leaves. The most popular home grown tea, called Liberty Tea, was derived from loosestrife plants, members of the primrose family that commonly grew in the fields and roadsides of New England.

Colonial women further supported anti-importation by refusing to purchase British textiles. Instead, they produced their own cloth and remade their families' old clothes. In 1768, a New York newspaper described the "glorious example" of two Newport women who "spun fully sixty yards of good fine linen cloth nearly a yard wide, besides taking care of a large family." By the time that the Revolution actually began, women were experts at "making do." In 1777, one woman told a British officer:

> I have retrenched every superfluous expense in my table and family. Tea I have not drunk since last Christmas, nor bought a new cap or gown since your defeat at Lexington: and, what I never did before, have learned to knit, and am now making stockings of wool for my servants: and this way do I throw in my mite for the public good. I know this, that as free I can die but once: but as a slave I shall not be worthy of life.

Besides supporting boycotts and nonimportation, women Patriots assisted in political actions against the British. They joined the Daughters of Liberty, who, along with the Sons of Liberty, held bonfire rallies, distributed anti-English propaganda, and hung tax collectors in effigy. The Boston Tea Party was initiated by Sarah Bradless Fulton, who was later known as the "Mother" of the famous event.

Some women organized active demonstrations on their own. In 1777, a group of Massachusetts women forcibly opened the warehouse of a merchant who was hoarding goods in order to sell them later at inflated wartime prices. It was reported that "a number of females, some say a hundred or more, assembled with a cart and trunks, marched down to the warehouse and demanded the keys, which he refused to deliver." One woman then grabbed him by his neck, pushed him into a cart, and seized the keys. After opening the warehouse, the women hoisted out hogsheads of coffee and drove off with them while a large group of men stood by in amazed silence.

Women pressured men in other ways to defy the British. Some young women refused to dance with or court men who had not declared their anti-English sentiments. Some wives denied their husbands "conjugal rights" until they swore their opposition to Great Britain. And a large number of women encouraged their husbands and sons to volunteer as members of the Continental Army.

Pushing their men toward the front lines meant great sacrifice for women who would now have to run the family farms and businesses by themselves, as well as to sell produce to supplement their husbands' irregular soldier's pay. When Abigail Adams's husband, John, urged her to "rouse your whole attention to the family, the stock, the farm, the dairy" in his absence, she responded by becoming an expert farm manager. It was her hope that, in time, she would have the "reputation of being as good a farmeress as my partner has of being a good statesman."

While single-handedly tending their families and farms, women Patriots organized women's associations that devoted untold hours to sewing clothes, rolling bandages, and preparing foodstuffs. In addition, they spent huge amounts of time and energy organizing charity fairs and other events to collect money for food, clothing, and sanitary supplies such as bandages for the army. In a fund-raising broadside printed in 1780, a Philadelphia woman explained that women were motivated by the "purest patriotism" in aspiring "to render themselves really useful." The campaign raised $30,000, which was used to purchase soldiers' shirts. In 1781, George Washington publicly praised the Ladies Association of Philadelphia for their fundraising efforts. They had "embellished" the American character, he stated, "by proving that the law of country is blended with those softer domestic virtues" of women. He added that these women deserved "an equal place with any who have preceded them in the walk of female patriotism."

Women not only created food and other goods, they also destroyed them rather than permit them to fall into the hands of the British. Rebecca Motte of South Carolina handed flaming arrows to soldiers to shoot at her home so that English soldiers would be forced to evacuate it. She quietly proclaimed, "I am gratified with the opportunity of contributing to the good of the country." She added, "I shall view the approaching scene with delight." Catherine Schuyler of Albany, New York, similarly burned fields of wheat to keep them from the enemy. Implementing a scorched earth policy, these and other women gladly destroyed their own homes and food supplies for the American cause.

None of these activities seem to diverge too far from the usual realm of female activities. But it is not widely recognized that women also collected lead, melted it down, and produced the shot used by the army. They manufactured and assembled arms. And they converted their businesses to wartime production. A Mrs. Proctor of Salem converted her tool factory to a rebel arsenal, while "Handy Betsy the Blacksmith" lent her expertise regarding cannon and other arms.

Other women became involved because of their technical skills. Mary Katherine Goddard, a leading printer and newspaper publisher in Baltimore, printed the official version of the Declaration of Independence in 1777. In 1775, she had been appointed postmaster of Baltimore and was probably the first woman to fill such a post. By the time of the Revolution, she was a successful and respected businessperson, an achievement recognized by the Continental Congress when it contracted with her for the Declaration.

Other women aided the Revolution by acting as saboteurs and spies. Lydia Darrah, a Quaker woman in Philadelphia, listened at the door of a room in her home, which British officers had taken over for meetings. When she heard attack orders read, she went through the British lines on the pretense of getting flour milled. She located an American officer to whom she entrusted her secret. A few days later, she placidly observed a British officer's despair at finding the American cannon mounted and prepared to receive his attack. "We have marched back here like a parcel of fools," he fumed.

Other attacks were thwarted by courageous women disguised as men. In Massachusetts, a group of women dressed themselves in their husbands' clothes and carried pitchforks in order to guard a nearby bridge. Here they unhorsed and searched a British courier. When they discovered dispatches concealed in his boot, they conducted him to the local jail for detention. In South Carolina, Elizabeth Marshall and her daughters-in-law also dressed as men. They, too, accosted a courier and seized his dispatches, thus blocking the passage of essential military intelligence.

Other women went directly to the front to offer their services. Mary Ludwig Hay McCauley was a camp cook, washwoman, and nurse. She was known as Molly Pitcher because she carried so many pails and pitchers of water to the men. When she saw her husband fall, she took over his cannon, keeping it in operation for the rest of the Battle of Monmouth. Soldiers remembered her as a warmhearted, energetic woman who swore volubly and chewed tobacco. In 1822, the Pennsylvania legislature rewarded her war service with a small pension.

Less well known is Margaret Corbin who fought and was wounded in the Battle of Fort Washington. Like Molly Pitcher, she followed her husband to the front, where she served as a nurse, cook, and washwoman. When he died at her side, Corbin filled his battle post until she was disabled by three grape shot that permanently cost her the use of one arm.

In 1779, she too received a small pension for her heroism. Known as "Captain Molly," Corbin was the first woman pensioner in the United States.

Deborah Sampson was a different type of revolutionary soldier. In 1782, she enlisted in the Continental forces under the name of Robert Shurtleff. Her unusual height, strong features, and great stamina protected her from discovery until she was hospitalized with a fever. After being exposed as an imposter, she was quickly discharged in 1783. She later wrote that she had "burst the tyrant bonds which held my sex in awe and clandestinely, or by stealth, grasped an opportunity, which custom and the world seemed to deny, as a natural privilege." She was granted a pension as a war veteran in 1792.

Scores of other women invaded the camps of the Continental Army, pledging to help in any way possible. Martha Washington, for example, wintered with her husband at Valley Forge. Here, she went from hut to hut carrying food to the sick and consoling the dying. Emily Greiger performed another type of service by volunteering to carry a message after the male soldiers in camp declined to do so. When she was detained by a British scout, Geiger ripped up the document and swallowed it. The next day she promptly delivered the message that she had quickly committed to memory. Yet another task that women often performed was combing the battlefields for the dead, whom they identified and gave proper burial.

This impressive description of women's war efforts actually only touches on their enormous involvement. Although a good deal of scholarly work has been done on revolutionary women, there is still much to be discovered about women who acted both as individuals and as organized groups to aid the cause of American liberty. Future research will be devoted not only to learning more about the women who worked at home and on the front but also to those who pledged their literary and intellectual talents to the war effort.

Phillis Wheatley, a black slave, was one such woman. She was purchased by a wealthy Boston merchant, John Wheatley, in 1761 as a personal servant. The Wheatleys soon recognized the young girl's nimble mind and gave her opportunities not usually given a slave. Phillis Wheatley became a Latin scholar, a poet, and a witty conversationalist. One of her most celebrated poems was "Ode to General Washington," published in the *Pennsylvania Magazine* in 1776. It identified her as a Patriot and gained her a personal invitation to visit General Washington's headquarters in Cambridge, Massachusetts.

Mercy Otis Warren was another patriotic poet. In addition, Warren was a historian, playwright, and propagandist of the Revolution. She turned her talents to political activism by writing three anti-British satirical plays during the war years. In the late 1770s, Warren began her major literary work, the three-volume *History of the Rise, Progress and Termination of the American Revolution,* which appeared in 1805. In 1790, Warren published a collection of verse entitled *Poems, Dramatic and Miscellaneous.* This volume included two pieces advocating human freedom. Warren's work indicated that she was not only a supporter of the principle of American liberty but was also an early enthusiast for the cause of female independence as well. She once commented to a friend that women should accept their "appointed subordination" only for the sake of "Order in Families," not due to any inferiority on their part.

During much of her lifetime, Warren was a close friend and frequent correspondent of Abigail Adams. According to historian Mary R. Beard, the voluminous correspondence of the two women is believed to have been the basis for the Committees of Correspondence, agencies for communicating insurrectionist ideas and actions from colony to colony. Beard pointed out that these two women discussed political events not only with each other but also with a number of men involved in the protest movement. Warren's and Adams's questions and comments elicited serious and often lengthy replies, which they then read to a group of people interested in discussing the issues involved.

Adams is today perhaps the best known woman of the Revolutionary era. Her letters to her husband, John, while he served in the Continental Congress have been quoted repeatedly by contemporary feminists. She is especially recognized for her attempts to extend the concepts of liberty and independence to other groups of people besides propertied white males.

In 1776, recognizing that a new form of government would have to be devised for the United States, Adams wrote to her husband: "In the new Code of Laws which I suppose it will be necessary for you to make I desire you would Remember the Ladies, and be more generous and favourable to them than your ancestors." She asked that he not "put such unlimited power in the hands of the Husbands" because "all Men would be tyrants if they could." She concluded by stating: "If perticular care and attention is not paid to the Ladies we are determined to foment a Rebellion, and will not ourselves bound by any Laws in which we have no voice, or Representation."

Adams was not asking for a social revolution in sex roles. She did not argue that women should vote or hold public office. She did not espouse equality for women or an abandonment of their domestic roles. Rather, Adams envisioned a legal system that would protect women from unlimited power in the hands of men.

John Adams responded to his wife's request in a joking manner. He wrote to her that he had heard that the Revolution had "loosened the bands of Government everywhere," even to the point of stirring up American Indians and black Americans. But, he added, her letter was "the first Intimation that another Tribe more numerous and powerfull than all the rest were grown discontented." Adams suggested to her friend Mercy Otis Warren that they petition the new Congress regarding the situation of women. She soon dropped her case with the statement to John: "I can not say that I think you very generous to the Ladies, for whilst you are proclaiming peace and good will to Men, Emancipating all Nations, you insist upon retaining an absolute power over Wives." Her last retort warned him that "we have it in our power not only to free ourselves but to subdue our Masters, and without violence throw both your natural and legal authority at our feet."

Adams's words were courageous yet in a sense empty in a day when women's rights and feminism were not major issues. She had few allies to back up her ideas and help her to mount the revolution of which she spoke. Yet she was still an effective reformer in certain ways. As her son, John Quincy Adams, wrote after her death, "her life gave the lie to every libel on her sex that was ever written." She was an accomplished business manager and self-proclaimed "farmeress" when John was away, which was a good deal of the time. Her wise investments and sound management provided the money to send her sons to Harvard, underwrite John's political career, finance the furnishing of several foreign legations and the newly constructed White House, and support the Adamses after John's retirement from the presidency.

Abigail Adams was also concerned with the anomaly of slavery. She was firmly convinced that the slave system destroyed the character of both individuals and society as a whole. In 1797, Adams sent a black servant boy to evening school. When her neighbors visited her to make known their objections, she strongly advocated the principle of "equality of Rights." Arguing that the young man was a freeman, Adams maintained that he had a right to an education. "Merely because his Face is Black, is he to be denied instruction? How is he to be qualified to procure a livelihood?" she asked. As a result of her impassioned defense of the young man's right to an education, the case was dropped.

Adams was the most visible, and probably the most vocal, woman of the Revolutionary era. But she clearly did not stand alone. There were many women who violated the dictates of the female role in order to follow their own interests and convictions. Whether they engaged in political activities, fought alongside men, wrote letters and tracts, or pursued other "unfeminine" activities, their actions challenged the model of American womanhood. Like the many assertive and irrepressible colonial women who preceded them, women of the war years displayed a high degree of independence of thought and spirit. Not content with the passivity and submissiveness that was widely believed to be their inherent nature, these women defied convention to follow their own desires, talents, and convictions.

In many cases, women were able to undertake "male" activities without much public or private censure. It was, after all, a time of national crisis that demanded the relaxation of the usual rules. Women who worked, fought, or wrote to help the cause of freedom were seen as patriotic and loyal to their country, if not to the dictates of their gender roles. Women who neglected the female sphere in order to participate in the larger public realm were indeed Patriots of the first order in many people's eyes.

It would seem logical to expect that these energetic and courageous women might be rewarded with some of the fruits of the Revolution. Perhaps they too would be granted a modicum of liberty and freedom. It also seems reasonable to expect that traditional beliefs regarding the weakness and inferiority of females would fall by the wayside as a consequence of these brave women's deeds. Surely, the post-Revolutionary years would be golden ones for American women. They would certainly expect to partake of the democracy that was so widely discussed throughout the new nation, especially since they had helped to secure it.

In recent years, historians of women have devoted a good deal of time to exploring whether the American Revolution did in fact produce any marked improvements in women's lives. They have collected and examined a wide variety of source materials in an attempt to assess the impact of the wartime period on women's roles. In fact, this research has resulted in a fascinating dialogue among historians who are unearthing contradictory findings. The issue of whether the Revolution helped or hindered the progress of American women is a provocative and stimulating debate.

In an essay in 1976, historian Joan Hoff-Wilson argued that the American Revolution brought about only an illusion of change for women. According to her, the war pushed America toward industrialism, a system that would move many women into factory jobs that were poorly paid and low in status. Women would thus lose whatever respect and autonomy they had as commanders of their households. Furthermore, the ideology of the new nation demanded "Republican Mothers," whose primary task was to train their sons for future citizenship and their daughters for future domesticity. In Hoff-Wilson's view, neither of women's new roles—that of factory worker or of Republican Mother—offered women any improvement in their positions. On the contrary, the female descendants of colonial women lost the economic authority and professional opportunities that their mothers and grandmothers had enjoyed.

In 1980, an important study by Mary Beth Norton challenged Hoff-Wilson's perception of the impact of the war on American women. In Norton's view, the Revolution had a positive effect on women's lives. The economic and social disruption that it created gave women the chance to take over farms, plantations, businesses, trades, and professions while men were involved in war-related duties. Norton's thorough examination of various types of evidence led her to the belief that the Revolution had an "indelible effect upon American women."

According to Norton, the changes were not to be found in the area of law and politics, but in women's private lives. Reform did not consist of the rewriting of legal codes, the granting of the vote to women, and the emergence of a strong feminist movement. Rather, it appeared in the reorganization of family structure and in women's aspirations. Norton maintained that the Revolution's effect on women could be determined only by an "analysis of women's private writings" rather than by an "examination of formal actions implemented by men."

Unlike Hoff-Wilson, Norton identified certain social and philosophical factors in the Revolution that encouraged the emergence of a generation of women with a strong sense of self. Moreover, women now lived in a world that offered them increased opportunities in education and other public activities. Norton observed that, while women of the Revolutionary era could not escape certain feminine standards, their domestic roles as wives and mothers were seen as having an impact upon the larger society. All Americans finally recognized the importance of motherhood. But, Norton added, the "republican definition of motherhood" would in itself eventually become a tremendous restriction on the development of American women. Norton concluded that, in the final analysis, "the legacy of the American Revolution for women was thus ambiguous."

Historian Linda K. Kerber presented similar findings in her investigation of how the Revolution affected women. "This is a difficult question to answer," Kerber wrote. "The war raised once again the old question of whether a woman could be a patriot—that is, an essentially political person—and it also raised the question of what form female patriotism might take." Basic assumptions about women were challenged. For example, coverture, the control of a married woman's property by her husband, suggested that she had little political identity of her own. If he fought for the Loyalist side, was she automatically a Loyalist as well? Was she responsible for her own crimes of treason and espionage? Could she, like the new nation, free herself of a burdensome master through divorce?

Kerber's study points out just how complex the situation of women actually was during the era of the Revolution and early nationhood. She emphasizes that, while many women experienced political involvement during the war itself, they soon learned that the new republic granted them few opportunities as political beings. Instead, women soon discovered that their value to the nation lay in Republican Motherhood, a concept that entrusted women with the morality of the nation's future citizens. According to Kerber, the conservative nature of the Revolution revealed itself in its failure to integrate women as true participants in the political community. Kerber noted: "It is possible to read the subsequent political history of women in America as the story of women's efforts to accomplish for themselves what the Revolution had failed to do."

This spirited discussion among historians of women is at once both intriguing and confusing. It offers few definitive answers to the question of how the Revolution changed women's status. It is unclear whether the war's ideology and economic impact caused improvement or decline in the condition of American women. Perhaps it is enough to acknowledge the incredibly complicated dimensions of the debate and to realize that there is no one answer to the many questions involved in it. Instead, a reasonable way to proceed in assessing the effect of the Revolution on women may be to recognize that the Revolution did cause change. Whether for better or for worse, women's lives were affected in many diverse areas by the war and the necessary aftermath of establishing a new nation.

Undoubtedly, the development of the concept of Republican, or Moral, Motherhood precipitated numerous alterations in women's roles during the late 1700s and early 1800s. During the colonial period, women had been viewed primarily as wives, helpmeets, and ornaments. Seventeenth- and eighteenth-century Americans did not idealize motherhood and often seemed unconcerned about it. Neither the helpmeet nor the ornament image of women placed any emphasis on mothering.

Maternal love was apparently taken for granted and was not considered to be a matter that needed direction or guidance. If anything, there was more discussion of fatherhood, since the father was the dominant member of the family. Because men worked in or near the home during the years of settlement, they were able to help rear their children. Mothers, on the other hand, were so busy with their many chores that they often relied on their husbands or other adult members of the household to care for their children.

By the end of the eighteenth century, however, these casual attitudes toward motherhood had changed dramatically. Topics such as breast-feeding, discipline, and the instilling of morality in young children now elicited the attention of ministers, authors of guidebooks, and physicians, among others. The Moral Mother was increasingly charged with nurturing loyal and effective citizens for the newly founded nation. She was responsible for protecting virtue and morality in the United States.

A number of social changes produced this modified perception of women's roles. Many men now worked away from the home, regularly leaving the care of children in the hands of women. The increasing availability of certain factory-produced goods began to alleviate the burden of incessant domestic labor, thus giving women more time for child care. And women read more than ever before, thus opening themselves to the rapidly growing literature on motherhood.

Perhaps many women also recognized that Republican Motherhood was in a way an upgrading of their inferior status. If so, such a realization would make it possible for them to accept its tenets willingly. The potential gain in prestige would also make it palatable to immigrant women who had little in their backgrounds to prepare them for notions of democracy and republicanism, especially in relation to mothering. Representing a growing diversity of cultural experiences, including eastern European, Jewish, and Catholic, immigrant women could identify with a role that granted them increased respect even if they did not yet understand its importance to their new country.

Not only women but men as well gradually accepted the idea that females were innately more loving and nurturing than males. During these years, mother's love was recognized as an inborn instinct. Maternal fondness and tenderness toward children were highly acclaimed. In summary, motherhood was idealized, romanticized, and sentimentalized by Americans who believed that the future of their new nation somehow depended on it.

Naturally, such drastic revisions in the image of women affected many elements of family life. Birthing itself was rapidly becoming a more complicated affair. By the time of the Revolution, an expectant mother's personal support network of family, friends, and midwife had largely been replaced by male physicians. The change was primarily due to the introduction of obstetrical forceps, as well as a growing concern about the welfare of the mother. Men moved into the field of midwifery by promising women help with difficult deliveries through the use of forceps, but eventually they took over almost all deliveries.

Dr. William Shippen of Philadelphia led the revolution in birthing techniques. After studying medicine, including midwifery, in London, Shippen returned to Philadelphia in 1762. He brought with him British standards concerning hospitals, medical training, and professionalism. At his urging, the only hospital in America, the Pennsylvania Hospital, initiated formal medical training and lectures in midwifery. Shippen became Professor of Anatomy, Surgery, and Midwifery. Since women were not admitted to formal medical training, they were denied knowledge of the forceps and were effectively limited in their practice as midwives. In 1763, Shippen's entry into the practice of midwifery in Philadelphia marked the beginning of male control of the delivery room.

By 1807, five medical schools in America offered courses in midwifery to male students. The increasing presence of trained male doctors in the delivery room transformed the birth process. Instruments and anesthesia came into regular use and the Caesarean section became a common emergency procedure. Because both wives and husbands often felt uncomfortable with the presence of a male, the doctor communicated with the pregnant woman through a nurse and avoided performing a vaginal examination. Standards of modesty and of delivery-room etiquette often caused improper medical care. Since the doctor usually worked under a sheet to avoid seeing the woman's body, accidents were common. A Dr. Dewees warned his students to be careful so that "no part of the mother is included in the locking of the blades" of the forceps. Apparently, this accident was common. Because the infant's umbilical cord also had to be cut under covers, newborn babies were sometimes mutilated as well. One story passed on to medical students told of a doctor who caught a newborn infant's penis in the blade of his scissors.

The whole aura of the birthing ceremony also changed. Rather than being an open event involving many supportive people, it was now conducted in a darkened room by a professional, aloof male physician. It was no longer a matter of nature but a disease that demanded scientific management. Oddly enough, the new strictures surrounding childbirth actually indicated more sympathy for the expectant mother, rather than less as it may appear. Changing attitudes toward the importance of motherhood called for more mothers to survive childbirth. In this sense, the entry of male physicians and instruments into the delivery room was a sign of the enhanced value of women.

Another consequence of the growing emphasis on motherhood was an interest in child-care practices. Manuals such as *Mother's Catechism and Maternal Instruction* appeared in large numbers. The prevailing view of children became less one of a miniature adult to be rescued from original sin and more one of a pliable and innocent being whose upbringing demanded specialized equipment, toys, and books. Children were increasingly seen as individuals. Thus, from the concept of motherhood came the concept of childhood.

A recent study of one Connecticut town during the end of the eighteenth and the beginning of the nineteenth century demonstrates that other significant modifications occurred in family structure and interaction during this period. The proportion of single women increased while family size slowly decreased. By 1796, for example, 8 percent of Baltimore's households were headed by women, two thirds of whom were widows and one third single women. An increase in the number of women in the general population created a more competitive marriage market in the closing decade of the eighteenth century. Widowed and single women supported themselves by working as seamstresses, laundresses, dyers, starchers, lace makers, and mantua makers. They also ran small businesses supplying groceries, dry goods, millinery, hardware, and other small goods.

Other changes were also evident. Women now controlled more personal and real property. They also applied for and were granted a large number of divorces, many more than men. This statistic might be interpreted as a consequence of an enhanced spirit of independence among women, along with a willingness on the part of society to take women's needs more seriously. Certainly, a new ideal of companionate marriage was developing. An anonymous article of the 1790s declared that an ideal marriage was one based on "mutual esteem, mutual friendship, mutual confidence, begirt about by mutual forbearance." Possibly the heightened worth of motherhood raised expectations regarding the contributions of men to marriage and family relationships. To protect their vulnerable children, women were perhaps no longer willing to endure their husband's adultery and alcoholism.

Another area of change that defies concrete explanation is the emergence of women artists. Although women continued to be heavily involved in the production of folk art and craft work within their homes, a number of them moved into the creation of more conventional works of art. They achieved this without the benefit of formal training or study abroad because these activities were believed to be unseemly for women.

Despite these limitations, several women gained public recognition for their pastel drawing during the late eighteenth century. Ruth Henshaw Bascom of Massachusetts was known for her pastel crayon portraits. Also proficient at needlework, Bascom reportedly never accepted money for any of her works. Sarah Perkins was a Connecticut pastelist who also produced portraits during the 1790s. Her work was cut short after she took charge of her seven brothers and sisters at the age of twenty, married a widower with five children, and then had four children of her own.

Other women artists worked in the medium of watercolor. Sophia Burpee sometimes combined her watercolors with embroidery. Ruby Devol Finch executed watercolor paintings, especially of the Parable of the Prodigal Son, as well as miniatures and family records. Like Finch, Mary Parke painted Biblical scenes in watercolors. Susanna Heebner of Pennsylvania also focused on religious themes. Her manuscript illuminations combined religious poetry, moral teachings, and brightly colored decorations.

Probably the best known female artist of this era was Sarah Miriam Peale. As the youngest daughter of James Peale, a renowned miniaturist and portrait painter, Peale had artistic advantages not available to other women. Trained by her father and her uncle—acclaimed natural history painter and portraitist, Charles Willson Peale—Sarah Peale became an accomplished portrait and still-life artist. Her clients included heads of state and generals. She was the first woman to have her work exhibited at the prestigious Pennsylvania Academy of the Fine Arts.

The public acceptance of these women as artists certainly indicates an important change in perceptions of women. Now accepting themselves as individuals who possessed at least a modicum of talent and ingenuity, women were expanding their horizons. Women began to blossom in other areas, particularly in education. The rhetoric of the 1780s and 1790s declared that reason and rationality were masculine qualities and not common among women. Yet, at the same time, many Americans believed that women must be educated for their roles as Republican Mothers. Several women took advantage of this ambivalence in order to argue for the improved education of women.

Judith Sargent Murray, an author and early feminist, was one of the first Americans to argue publicly for increased educational opportunities for women. In 1779, writing under the pen name of Constantia, Murray declared that men and women had equal minds that deserved equivalent educations. "Are women deficient in reason?" she asked. "We can only reason from what we know, and if an opportunity of acquiring knowledge hath been denied us, the inferiority of our sex cannot fairly be deduced from thence." If women were "allowed an equality of acquirements" in the realm of education, they would "meet on even ground" in their achievements.

At the same time, Abigail Adams, in her letters to her husband, was exploring the meaning of the Revolution for women's education. After reading the Declaration of Independence, Adams understood that women's primary duty was to cultivate wisdom and loyalty in their children, thus preserving virtues necessary to a free republic. But how would women train "Heroes, Statesmen and Philosophers," she wondered, if they themselves were not "learned." In 1778, she reminded John of the "trifling narrow contracted Education" of women in the new United States. "You need not be told," she wrote, "how much female Education is neglected, nor how fashionable it has been to ridicule Female learning." Adams continued to worry about the matter and, by 1787, concluded that women were "rational Beings," whose minds "might with propriety receive the highest possible cultivation." Adams recognized that an educated woman would "draw upon herself the jealousy of the Men and the envy of the Women," but she believed that the only "way to remedy this evil" was "by increasing the number of accomplished women," thus forcing their acceptance by society.

As women's education became an ongoing debate, it was obvious that most Americans believed that the new republican woman should be rational, competent, and self-reliant. As Linda Kerber has pointed out, women were now to be educated for the good of the republic. This view did not support "intellectual" women or the departure of women from the home as their primary sphere. Rather, it emphasized the idea that women's duties in the home had achieved a new significance. The celebrated Dr. Benjamin Rush of Philadelphia explained it this way: "Let the ladies of a country be educated properly and they will not only make and administer its laws, but form its manners and character."

In 1787, Rush presented a model curriculum for republican women to the board of visitors of the Young Ladies Academy of Philadelphia. He maintained that "female education should be accommodated to the state of society, manners, and government of the country in which it is conducted." The course of study of this academy, which claimed to be the first of its kind chartered in the United States when it opened in 1787, included reading, writing, arithmetic, English grammar, composition, rhetoric, and geography. The curriculum represented an alteration in ideas regarding women. Prominent men had, for the first time, devoted their time and energy to advocate the concept of a sound education for women.

Yet addresses by the academy's graduates reflected these young women's acceptance of the *status quo*. "I believe I must give up all pretensions to profundity," one stated, "for I am more at home in my female character." Only a few of these women made any mention of equal education and widening the accepted female sphere. But the academy's founders did not intend it "as constituting an Era altogether new." Instead, there is strong evidence that the school's founders wanted to lessen women's discontent while improving the education of the mothers of the new country's future citizens.

In the South, too, women were taking advantage of increased educational opportunities. Women's academies were at the center of the movement away from superficial education in "female accomplishments" to more solid training in subjects that would contribute to women becoming more effective mothers and more informed citizens. In 1805, a Virginia planter requested that his daughter send him a complete account of her academy education: "It is not enough for me to know that you make as much progress in your French and Geography as you possibly can! I wish to know precisely what that progress is—I wish to know how each day is employed—what proportion is devoted to study, to writing, to cyphering, to reading, to sewing, to amusement, to idleness." Southern women flocked to academies in order to gain, if not equality, at least an improved quality of life as wives, mothers, and plantation mistresses.

During the closing decades of the 1700s and the opening years of the 1800s, women asserted themselves not only in educational institutions but in religious ones as well. Although a woman's ability to reason was often questioned, her sense of piety was not. During the early 1700s, male church membership had begun to decline. By the Revolutionary era, the number of women church members far outnumbered men. Soon most congregations had a majority of female members. Religious activity offered women a voice and a role, however limited it might be. Women, subordinate in other areas of life, discovered an opportunity to express themselves in the churches. During the 1770s, Mother Ann Lee even promoted a new sect, Shakerism. And during the 1780s, revivalist Jemima Wilkinson attracted numerous followers.

As church audiences became largely female, ministers found it necessary to "feminize" their message to meet the needs of their listeners. Clergymen turned their attention to topics of concern to women, such as the family, public and private morality, the refinement of society, and missionary endeavors. They also stressed the crucial role of godly mothers and the importance of women's morality, thus adding the church's voice to the growing emphasis on motherhood.

When the Second Great Awakening occurred in the late 1790s, women were in its forefront. As religious, emotional, and highly moral beings, they saw themselves as the inculcators of virtue not only in children but in men as well. They actively recruited men for conversion, an act that implied the superiority of their female religious nature. Women also openly expressed anger against authority, particularly that of ungodly men and controlling ministers. Through religion, women vented the tensions caused by other limitations on their lives.

The political realm was one such source of frustration for women. They soon learned that the brave statements regarding freedom and liberty for all contained in the Declaration of Independence did not include them. John Adams argued that, while women were theoretically part of the new government of the United States, their influence was exercised in the home rather than in any public political capacity. Thomas Jefferson, the author of the Declaration, believed that "the tender breasts of ladies were not formed for political convulsion." Consequently, republican women found that the United States Constitution included no rights or protections for them. Women received no new legal codes nor were they freed from coverture and the limitations of marital unity. They had no representatives in governing bodies nor any emissaries or planks in the platforms of the first political parties. Their occasional right to vote in some local and state elections was exercised for the last time in 1807 in New Jersey.

Clearly, the many political ramifications of the Revolution and the new nation's government did not extend to women. Even in such egalitarian frontier regions as those along the Cumberland River, women were not granted political privileges during the 1780s and 1790s. They were not rewarded with increased opportunities, although their effort and energy was crucial in expanding the new country toward the west and south.

These women aided the formation of the new states entering the union after the Revolution—Kentucky in 1792, Tennessee in 1796, and Ohio in 1803.

Frontierswomen fought alongside their men in wresting the land from its native owners, worked to clear the land with oxen, mules, horses, and primitive machinery, and struggled to raise their children as educated "proper" people. When they lost their men, many frontierswomen continued to work on their own. It has been estimated that almost two thirds of early women settlers in Tennessee alone were widowed by Indian wars by the 1790s. Yet few left the frontier to live with families in the more settled eastern regions. Widowed in 1781, Leah Lucas stayed on the Cumberland frontier, farming the family land and raising five children.

Other women who did have husbands also learned to manage farms, children, and crises on their own while their men were absent on long trips. Married to hunters, traders, trappers, surveyors, and politicians, Cumberland women stayed home and minded the family enterprise. Daniel Smith, for example, was gone from his family more than a year when he helped to survey the North Carolina-Virginia line in 1779–1780. Thus, women often tilled the fields, built houses and out-buildings, bred animals, cared for their children, and did a multitude of heavy tasks.

Even when men were on the scene to care for the fields and stock, frontierswomen's work was extensive and exhausting. A woman managed the house, children, and dairy—all complex tasks requiring training and skill. Women's labor and management abilities were often recognized by their menfolk in their wills, which commonly left property to a spouse and assigned a wife as executrix. There was also a good deal of respect given to women, but they were not widely encouraged to explore new roles in the public arena.

American Indian women fared even worse in the new nation of the Revolutionary period than did Euro-American women. Along with Indian men, native women suffered because of white expansionism. As the white population moved westward, it became increasingly impatient with native concepts of communal landholding. Puzzled by the Indian belief that land belonged to everyone and thus could not be transferred to an individual through a piece of paper, whites resorted to threats and trickery to get Indians to agree to land sales. Convinced of the validity of "private property"—and of their God-given right to the land—whites pushed Indians farther and farther west.

Most whites seemed to overlook or ignore the fact that the brisk trade conducted with Indians significantly aided the economic development of the American frontier. They minimized Indians' contributions to western development as porters, laborers, traders in furs and other goods, guides, bridge builders, explorers of routes, and suppliers of food and other necessary commodities to white migrants. Because most Indians preferred their own cultures and refused to assimilate to white ways, whites destroyed them or pushed them farther westward.

This displacement of American Indians was accompanied by white exploitation of native women. As a case in point, the American fur trade weakened the status and power of Indian women by utilizing them as poorly paid and low-status interpreters, workers, and liaisons. The "civilization" that the fur traders carried to native women included venereal disease, prostitution, and abandonment by white husbands. At the same time, factory-produced goods began to undermine the use of items such as textiles and pottery produced by native women. And white attitudes regarding the inferiority of women denied Indian women any recognition or reward for the significant role that they played in the development of the fur trade itself.

Thus, the importance of Indian women to their particular societies gradually diminished. Like white women, they were increasingly relegated to the domestic sphere. Opportunities for women to become political leaders of their communities, serve as shamans or warriors, and actively engage in trade began to decrease. In Iroquois society, for instance, a group of female elders had long served as sachems on tribal councils, the most powerful ruling body. White leaders, however, disapproved of such power in the hands of women and now effectively denied it to Iroquois women by refusing to deal with them. Under the matrilineal system of the Cherokee, women held property, kept their children in case of a divorce, and decided whether captives would be adopted or punished. As a result of intermarriage with whites and the United States government's "civilization" policy, the Cherokee were encouraged to abandon this arrangement in favor of a patrilineal pattern of inheritance. Cherokee women had lost further power by 1800, when a depleted game supply caused Cherokee men and African slaves to take over the agricultural tasks that belonged to women.

Unlike their white counterparts, Indian women did not have a "republic" for which to labor within the home. In addition, they were neither "virtuous" nor moral in white eyes and were becoming less so in the Indian view as well. Their possibilities for achievement were diminishing and were not being replaced by prominence as mothers. By the early years of the 1800s, the situation of Indian women bore less resemblance to that of white women than ever.

Of course, white society was largely unconcerned about the position of American Indian women. The native women who commanded the attention of whites continued to be those that helped them to achieve their ends. Thus, Sacajawea, an Idaho Shoshoni, gained historical fame among whites when she aided the Lewis and Clark expedition as an interpreter and guide between 1804 and 1806. In another case, Marie Dorion, an Iowa Indian, was remembered as the only woman on the famed expedition to Astoria (1811–1812) on the Columbia River and as an Indian who warned whites of a native attack. It is from the shackles of such stereotypes that Indian women's history is currently struggling to emerge.

Like American Indian women, black women were also objects of exploitation by whites. With the growth of industrialization in the North and the cotton culture in the South after the Revolution, black slavery gradually declined in the northern states while it became dominant in the southern ones. As profits from cotton began to rise, white slaveowners intensified their efforts to extract the most labor possible from black slave women. After Congress abolished the slave trade in 1808, black women were also expected to become "breeders," that is, to produce as many slave children as possible. Prizes, promises of freedom, and other rewards were frequently offered to slave women who bore ten or more children.

Black slave women also labored as nursemaids, midwives, domestic servants, and field hands. On the larger plantations, they served as seamstresses, nurses, poultrymaids, and dairymaids. Since the number of trades and crafts that black women were allowed to pursue were limited, compared to those open to black slave men who worked as blacksmiths, coopers, overseers, and in other similar capacities, more women worked in the fields than did men. The black female field hand was routinely expected to perform domestic tasks as well. One Virginia planter of the late 1700s described a favored slave as "a stout able field wench and an exceedingly good washer and ironer."

These black women were regarded as chattels rather than human beings. They were listed in property inventories of plantations by first name, age, and monetary value. On the auction block, they were scrutinized much like livestock. At one slave sale, a small buyer "took one of the prettiest women by the chin and opened her mouth to see the state of her gums and teeth, with no more ceremony than if she had been a horse."

In spite of the indignities and degradation of the slave system, black women provided the glue that held slave families together. Familial ties were extremely important to black slaves; yet they lived with the constant threat of separation from their kin. Slaves continually protested against their inability to establish families and preserve family units. In 1774, a group of Massachusetts slaves petitioned the state legislature for their freedom, stressing the destructive nature of slavery on family life: "How can a slave perform the duties of husband to wife or a parent to a child? How can a husband leave his master to work and cleave to his wife? How can the wife submit to her husband in all things?" Although

Massachusetts and other northern states manumitted their slaves, the southern slave system continued to exploit black women while often wrenching their families from them.

One change that the Revolution did bring about for black Americans was the hope of eventual abolition from their slave status. During the war itself, the presence of British armies encouraged slaves to escape their owners. Moreover, the British often harbored runaway slaves and granted them freedom as a means of weakening the efforts of southern Patriots. After the war, the British transported many slaves who had joined them to Nova Scotia in Canada. These former slaves frequently escaped in family groups that included women and children. Over half of the twenty-three slaves who fled Thomas Jefferson's Virginia plantation during the war were women and girls.

At the war's conclusion, many Americans supported the abolition of slavery. A number of slaveowners in the upper South chose to free their slaves in a burst of abolitionist enthusiasm. This move created a free black population that included many women. Other Americans began to form abolitionist societies. As long-time opponents of slavery, the Quakers were in the forefront of this activity. Abolitionist societies, organized in Philadelphia and elsewhere in the middle states, sought to convince Americans that their freedom should extend to blacks. Using the Declaration of Independence as a basis, they claimed that liberty for one and all should transcend distinctions of color. And several states passed abolition provisions. The Massachusetts Constitution of 1780, for instance, included a Declaration of Rights stating that "all men are born free and equal." Under this provision such slaves as Elizabeth Freeman (also known as Mum Bett) finally received liberation from their slave status.

Other Americans argued that black slaves who participated in the Revolution should be rewarded with their freedom. Yet, in practice, this policy was seldom implemented. A black woman who served as a bullet runner for American troops remained a slave until she was nearly 80, at which time she escaped to Canada. Another black woman who served a colonel for forty years was denied her impassioned plea for freedom in 1782.

Pennsylvania was a leader in attempting to erase the contradictions between the nation's freedom and the servitude of some of its citizens. During the Revolution, Pennsylvania passed the Gradual Abolition Law which in turn led to an increase in the state's black population. The Census of 1790 recorded 10,301 blacks in Pennsylvania—6,540 free and 3,761 slaves. But the state's abolition provisions attracted such an influx of blacks, many via the early Underground Railroad, that the total had jumped 176 percent by 1800. By 1800, Pennsylvania's black population numbered 16,270—14,564 free and 1,706 slaves.

The situation of free black women in Pennsylvania did not markedly improve as a result of the experiment in gradual abolition. They were often denied employment. When employed, they worked on farms or as domestic servants for impossibly low wages. And they lived with the ever-present fear of being captured and sold into slavery.

Evidently, the Revolution had not dramatically altered the lives of women—white, Indian, or black—in any major way. They were still viewed and treated largely in prejudicial and discriminatory terms. The writings in the 1780s of two male commentators illustrate the ways which most Americans viewed native, black, and white women during the late eighteenth century. The perceptions that they recorded were common and are extremely useful in gaining insight into women's historical experiences. The ideas of these two educated, sophisticated men distinctly reveal the stronghold that images and stereotypes of women and womanhood had over people's minds in this era.

One of these writers was Thomas Jefferson. Regarding Indian women, Jefferson noted that they were forced to submit to "unjust drudgery," as was the "case with every barbarous people." They bore fewer children than white women, for, as "with all animals, if the female be badly fed, or not fed at all, her young perish." To Jefferson, such "obstacles of want" were simply nature's way of limiting "the multiplication of wild animals." He concluded that, when married to a white man, an Indian woman who was fed properly, exempted from "excessive drudgery," and protected from danger could bear as many children as white women. His view, like that of most white Americans at the time, was based more on prejudice and ignorance than knowledge.

Jefferson displayed a similar bias when he turned his attention to black women. He lamented the absence of "flowing hair" and "symmetry of form" in black women as compared with whites. Moreover, "the veil of black" gave their faces an "eternal monotony" that contrasted unfavorably with the "fine mixtures of red and white, the expressions of every passion by greater or less suffusions of color" that appeared in white women's faces. Observing that blacks slept frequently, he explained that an "animal whose body is at rest, and who does not reflect, must be disposed to sleep of course." Jefferson could not identify an occasion when a black "had uttered a thought above the level of plain narration," nor displayed "even an elementary trait of painting or sculpture." He dismissed Phillis Wheatley as an example of religious zeal, rather than of talent. "The compositions published under her name are below the dignity of criticism," he concluded.

Given the fact that Jefferson was considered a democratic, liberal thinker, his attitudes seem rather prejudiced, even for his time. If these were the ideas of a sophisticated, well-educated liberal, then the chances are that the mass of Americans were even more unenlightened. Jefferson's descriptions of American Indian and black American women certainly do not indicate the existence of a crucible of liberty for them.

The second writer was Hector St. John de Crèvecoeur, a New York farmer of French background, who demonstrated a very different set of prejudices in his discussion of white women in America. The images of his own wife that inspired his love focus upon her spinning, knitting, or nursing a child. He claimed that, like him, American men did not expect a dowry with a wife, for they realized that a "wife's fortune consists principally in her future economy, modesty, and skillful management." According to Crèvecoeur, if a farmer were "blessed with a good wife," he had the opportunity to live better than "any people of the same rank on the globe."

Several significant points emerge from the writings of these two influential men. Their essays discuss white women largely in terms of their domestic roles and native and black women primarily in terms of their race. They extol white women's contributions to the nation and denigrate those of native and black women. And they show that even educated, liberal observers were deeply affected by prevailing stereotypes of women.

Clearly, women's image and "sphere" had been tested by the confusions created by the American Revolution and the forming of the new nation. Changes in thinking regarding women included the ideal of companionate marriage, legitimacy of women's education, an increased respect for motherhood, and talk of enhanced self-esteem for women. Yet the traditional conception of women solely as wives and mothers had not only survived, but had expanded its dimensions and increased its influence. At the same time, however, many women had grown restive with the restrictions on their lives and had begun to question their validity.

This ambivalent situation would soon be disrupted by two major occurrences—the Industrial Revolution and the westward movement—which would alter both the stereotypes and the actuality of American women's lives. The Industrial Revolution, already well on its way by 1800, along with growing westward migration marked by the flow of people toward the Mississippi River after the Revolution, would soon revise the parameters of the model. How these two movements affected both the image and the reality of women's lives is the next chapter in the story of the experiences of American women.

SUGGESTIONS FOR FURTHER READING

Akers, Charles W. *Abigail Adams: An American Woman.* Boston: Little, Brown and Company, 1980.

Berkin, Carol Ruth, and Mary Beth Norton, eds. *Women of America: A History.* Boston: Houghton Mifflin, 1979. Part II, 3.

Bloch, Ruth H. "American Feminine Ideals in Transition: The Rise of the Moral Mother, 1785–1815." *Feminist Studies* 4 (June 1978): 101–126.

Bogdan, Janet. "Care or Cure: Childbirth Practices in Nineteenth Century America." *Feminist Studies* 3 (June 1978): 92–99.

Chambers - Schiller, Lee Virginia. *Liberty, A Better Husband: Single Women in America, The Generations of 1780–1840.* New Haven: Yale University Press, 1984.

Clark, Ella E., and Margot Edmonds. *Sacagawea of the Lewis and Clark Expedition.* Berkeley and Los Angeles: University of California Press, 1979.

Clinton, Catharine. *The Other Civil War: Women in the Nineteenth Century.* New York: Hill and Wang, 1984. Chapter 1.

———. "Equally Their Due: The Education of the Planter Daughter in the Early Republic." *Journal of the Early Republic* 2 (Spring 1982): 39–60.

Cody, Cheryll Ann. "Naming, Kinship and Estate Disposal: Notes on Slave Family Life on a South Carolina Plantation, 1786–1833." *William and Mary Quarterly* 39 (January 1982): 192–211.

Dewhurst, C. Kurt, Betty MacDowell, and Marsha MacDowell. *Artists in Aprons: Folk Art by American Women.* New York: E. P. Dutton, 1979.

Dye, Nancy Schrom. "History of Childbirth in America." *Signs* 6 (Autumn 1980): 97–108.

Friedman, Jean E., and William G. Shade, eds. *Our American Sisters: Women in American Life and Thought.* Lexington, MA: D. C. Heath and Company, 1982). Part I, Nos. 5 and 6.

James, Edward T., ed. *Notable American Women, 1607–1905: A Biographical Dictionary.* Cambridge, MA: Belknap Press, 1971.

Kerber, Linda K. *Women of the Republic: Intellect and Ideology in Revolutionary America.* Chapel Hill: University of North Carolina Press, 1980.

Newman, Debra L. "Black Women in the Era of the American Revolution in Pennsylvania." *Journal of Negro History* 61 (July 1976): 276–289.

Niethammer, Carolyn. *Daughters of the Earth: The Lives and Legends of American Indian Women.* New York: Macmillan Publishing Company, 1977.

Norton, Mary Beth. *Liberty's Daughters: The Revolutionary Experience of American Women, 1750–1800.* Boston: Little, Brown and Company, 1980.

Perdue, Theda. *Slavery and the Evolution of Cherokee Society, 1540–1866.* Knoxville: University of Tennessee Press, 1979.

Sheils, Richard D. "The Feminization of American Congregationalism, 1730–1835." *American Quarterly* 33 (Spring 1981): 46–62.

Smith, Daniel Blake. "The Study of the Family in Early America: Trends, Problems, and Prospects." *William and Mary Quarterly* 39 (January 1982): 3–28.

Utley, Beverly. "Brave Women." *American History Illustrated* 3 (1968): 10–18.

Van Kirk, Sylvia. *Many Tender Ties: Women in Fur-Trade Society, 1670–1870.* Norman: University of Oklahoma Press, 1983.

Woloch, Nancy. *Women and the American Experience.* New York: Alfred A. Knopf, 1984. Chapters 3–4.

Wertz, Richard W., and Dorothy C. Wertz. *Lying-In*. New York: Free Press, 1977.

Wright, Mary C. "Economic Development and Native American Women in the Early Nineteenth Century." *American Quarterly* 33 (Winter 1981): 525–536.

Western artist W. H. D. Koerner created this painting of a westering woman in 1921.
Madonna of the Prairie *captures one popular and enduring image of frontierswomen.*
Courtesy of the Buffalo Bill Historical Center, Cody, Wyoming.

CHAPTER 3

The Cult of True Womanhood: Industrial and Westward Expansion 1816–1837

BY the second decade of the nineteenth century, the United States was caught up in a fever of growth and expansion. A "boom psychology" encouraged capitalists to invest in new industries, people to flock to American cities from the countryside and from other countries in search of jobs, and thousands of others to stream across the Appalachian Mountains toward the beckoning frontier. Industrialization and the westward migration wrought dramatic changes in the face of the new nation between 1816 and 1837.

Prevailing images and realities of women's lives experienced widespread alterations as well. The customary image of women as primarily wives and mothers not only persisted, but was enhanced by a highly developed doctrine of woman's sphere. Yet, at the same time, the actual activities and employment of women were challenging the traditional concept of separate spheres. By the time of the Panic of 1837—a turning point in the nation's history—the invented American woman appeared to be solid on the surface but, upon closer examination, was actually in a state of flux. All that was certain was that industrial and westward expansion had called the model of American womanhood into serious question.

American women felt the impact of the era's growth in many ways, not all of them positive. In 1816, the appointment of the first congressional committee to study women laborers recognized the widereaching effects of industrialization. Among other things, industrialization transformed household production, created social classes of women, and drew huge numbers of women from their homes into paid employment. These changes, along with their attendant problems, would eventually cause dissatisfied American women to challenge the image of women that restricted their lives.

The story begins in 1789, when the first factory for carding and spinning yarn in America was established in Rhode Island. Because most men were engaged in agriculture, proponents of the American factory system suggested hiring women. They did not want to destroy agriculture in order to develop industry. Besides, it seemed natural for women, who had spun and woven in their own homes, to move their customary work into a factory setting. In his Report on Manufacturers of 1791, Secretary of the Treasury Alexander Hamilton advocated factory employment for women because it made development of the new system possible "without taking men from the fields." He added that this would also render women "more useful than they otherwise would be," while farms would prosper as a result of the income brought in by the "increased industry" of farm wives and daughters.

These arguments multiplied many times over during the following years. Tench Coxe, an avid supporter of manufacturing, argued that "the portions of time of housewives and young women which were not occupied with family affairs could be profitably filled up" by factory work. This view soon expanded to include the claim that a new factory was actually a blessing to a community because it furnished employment for its women. A few years later, it was added that women were "kept out of vice simply by being employed and instead of being destitute provided with an abundance for a comfortable subsistence." In 1822, Philadelphia philanthropist Mathew Carey stated that, without the factory, young women would lack "employment and spend their time perniciously—a burden to their parents and society—trained up to vicious courses." But with factory employment, they were "happily preserved from idleness and its attendant vices and crimes."

It is unclear how instrumental these arguments were in propelling women into factories. Women did enter such employment in large numbers, but it was probably because of the increasing need that farm families had for cash income during the early 1800s. The congressional committee of 1816 identified 100,000 industrial workers in the United States, two out of three of whom were female. By 1828, 9 out of 10 textile workers in New England were female.

Thousands of young farm women in New England left their families to relocate in the new mill towns. The best known of these factory villages was Lowell, Massachusetts. Here, women workers lived together in company-owned boardinghouses. Often, these women sent part of their meager wages home to their families, while their brothers remained on the farm to provide agricultural labor or attended college, often on their sister's earnings. As a result of their paid employment, daughters were now seen as a "blessing to the farmer," rather than a liability.

The Lowell women commonly worked twelve to fourteen hours a day, tending two or more machines for about $2.00 a week. They were offered various cultural benefits such as libraries and participation in the company-sponsored literary journal, *The Lowell Offering*. Although the boardinghouses were supervised by matrons, the factory women enjoyed a certain amount of independence. Lowell was frequently held up as a model factory village with ideal working and living conditions.

As early as the mid-1820s, however, it was becoming clear that all was not well among textile operatives. Although wages had not increased, the work pace had. Hours were still long, and working conditions were worsening. Boardinghouses were overcrowded, and goods in the company-owned stores were expensive. In 1824, a group of women protested against low wages and bad conditions by walking out of a mill in Pawtucket, Rhode Island. Many other strikes, or "turnouts," followed in other areas. These culminated at Lowell itself in the 1840s when the first women's labor organization, the Lowell Female Reform Association, under the leadership of Sarah Bagley, began a crusade for a ten-hour workday. The journal of this reform organization, *Voice of Industry*, complained about an increased work pace and other problems while asking the Massachusetts legislature to investigate conditions in the mills.

Women workers did not make much progress with these protests. After all, they were expendable because there were always more young women or, by the 1840s, Irish immigrants willing to fill their places. Women had difficulty supporting labor organizations on their low wages. And, as women, they were denied knowledge of and access to avenues of power such as public officeholding.

Despite the continued problems associated with factory employment, women who found it necessary to help support their families moved to industrial occupations in large numbers. By the 1820s and 1830s, many of these women workers were foreign born. Young, unmarried immigrant women were routinely expected to help support their families. Almost 60 percent of young, single Irish women worked with German and other groups following similar employment patterns to a lesser extent. Even in conservative Italian families, daughters were often expected to work as a temporary relief for an overburdened family budget. And in many Jewish families, both single and married women worked so that their men could continue the much revered religious study of the Torah, especially if they aspired to the respected position of Rabbi.

Women worked primarily in textile factories, cotton mills, shoe factories, and the needle trades. They were typed as "lady operatives" who worked cheaply and could be hired and fired as needed. Yet many women preferred the factory over teaching, sewing, and domestic service, all of which paid less. In 1839, mill worker Malenda Edwards claimed that, "There are very many young ladies at work in the factories that have given up millinery dressmaking and school-keeping for to work in the mill."

Poor pay, bad working conditions, long hours, low status, and inability to organize plagued women factory workers and was even worse for the numerous women who worked in their homes producing parts to be assembled in factories. They were paid "piecework" wages, a minimal fee per part. As a case in point, the country's largest women's shoe factory, located in Lynn, Massachusetts, depended on the needle skills of women pieceworkers to bind or to stitch shoe uppers in their homes. Women also worked at home as seamstresses. After observing Philadelphia seamstresses in 1829, one commentator noted: "It takes great expertness and increasing industry from sunrise to 10 and 11 at night, constant employment which few of them have, to earn a dollar and a half per week."

Perhaps the most underpaid of all women workers were domestic servants. Many early American homes had included "hired help," who were often regarded as members of the family and assisted with all of the ongoing domestic tasks. In the eighteenth century, help was largely replaced by domestics who were seen as servants and assigned specific menial chores performed apart from family members. The large influx of immigrants, especially Irish, provided a source of needy, untrained women for the domestic service market at extremely low wages. In 1837, one observer commented that "a woman who goes out to wash works as hard in proportion as a wood sawyer or a coal heaver, but she is not generally able to make more than half as much for a day's work."

Given the difficulties of women's labor, it is probably not surprising that many women became prostitutes. Many destitute seamstresses and servants turned to this relatively lucrative pursuit in New York and other cities. Immigrant and farm girls were often lured into "white slavery" by operators of brothels. Despite its growth, neither prostitution nor the resulting spread of venereal disease was publicly discussed, acknowledged or even known during these years.

The various types of women workers constituted a new female working class. Gerda Lerner has pointed out, however, that these working women were both isolated and disenfranchised. The issues in which they were interested related to their own immediate situations and included better pay and improved working conditions. Because questions concerning equality, education, and property ownership were not relevant to their lives, they seldom identified with early feminists who advocated reform in these areas. Because of the fluidity of the women's labor market and the scattered nature of their workplaces, mill girls probably even lacked a collective identity.

Although many women became paid workers by the 1830s, more women remained in their homes than not. Here they worked at such customary chores as cooking, food processing, and child care. Frequently, women now exchanged money for many of the goods that they needed instead of producing them. Some women were relieved of certain tasks by the presence of domestic servants. But in many other cases, especially on farms, women continued to labor as domestic artisans and occasionally as field helpers.

Women who remained in their homes did so for a variety of reasons. Many could afford to stay home and devote themselves to the care of their families. The emphasis that the concept of Republican Motherhood placed on child rearing convinced such women that child care should be their first duty. They believed that this involved providing such services as establishing a moral climate for their children or offering moral support for employed members of the family. Frequently, professional and entrepreneurial men preferred to have their wives and daughters remain at home as symbols of their own ability to support a family. When possible, these men enhanced their images of success by hiring domestic servants and nursemaids to aid their wives.

In the South, planters similarly desired their wives to remain within the home and provided black slaves as servants and nurses. The southern woman was restricted by the Cult of White Womanhood, which characterized women as fragile, delicate creatures in need of protection and guidance. In 1854, social theorist George Fitzhugh claimed that, "Women, like children, have but one right, and that is the right to protection." He added that "the right to protection involved the right to obey," and, "if she be obedient, she stands little danger of maltreatment."

Thus middle- and upper-class American women were given a modicum of leisure. This woman was regarded as a "lady," who labored neither at a job nor at home. Her many responsibilities in managing home, children, and servants were overlooked. It was generally assumed that the availability of servants and slaves, combined with factory-produced goods, made the lady of leisure a reality.

In order to help ladies understand and to shape their roles, lifestyles, and behavior, prescriptive literature, such as guidebooks and etiquette manuals, began to flow from the presses. One popular guide cautioned ladies to keep any learning that they might have a secret, "especially from the men, who generally look with a jealous and malignant eye on a woman of great parts and cultivated understanding." Another advised them to turn their talents to instilling virtue in children, men, and servants. Others urged the need for a woman to marry, both for happiness and economic survival. "Her family is the source of all her joy," one proclaimed.

Extensive discussion ensued regarding the "proper spheres of the sexes." It was generally agreed that men were to provide income and take care of public affairs. Women were to establish homes that would "dispel the gloom and restore the ease and comfort" of men after long days spent coping with weighty matters. The world was to be men's undisputed realm, while the home belonged to women. In this system, such fashionable "accomplishments" as playing the piano and speaking French became more important than ever in attracting a "suitable" husband. One young lady duly learned all the appropriate graces, including how to curtsy and dance. When she was about to wed, her mother reminded her that now it would be her "first care to please and make your husband happy."

Raising children also required the lady's attention. The importance of the American mother was celebrated by the expanding publishing industry. Mothers were now seen as the sole shapers of values and character. They were exhorted to mold and train their children into virtuous and responsible people. Women were further cautioned to "let thy children be the darlings of thy tenderness." It was widely assumed that women's maternal love, now believed to be innate, would guide them in the proper disposal of their motherly duties.

Although only a small proportion of women in industrial America actually were leisure ladies, the concept was soon elevated to the status of ideology. It went hand in hand with what historian Barbara Welter has termed the Cult of True Womanhood. This ideology preached four cardinal virtues—piety, purity, submissiveness, and domesticity—as the goals of all true women. In a sense, the ideals of true womanhood offered women a vehicle through which they might become, or at least emulate, ladies.

The image of the "leisure lady" quickly became the ideal of femininity. It decreed that the home was the woman's domain and that she ruled it totally. Her only proper sphere was the care of that home and its inhabitants. Unrelated vocations or activities would only lead her away from the path of true womanhood.

Although ladies were on the other end of the social scale from mill girls and other women workers, they, too, were isolated and disenfranchised. But, unlike their counterparts in the factories, many ladies did care about such topics as education and property ownership because they were extremely important to their own lives. Although women generally found the endeavor of being ladies amusing for a few years, many of them gradually turned to an examination of these serious issues. In practical terms, ladies had more time than female laborers to reflect upon their ills. They also came together through social activities and so could discuss their problems in small groups. And they had the education, money, and time to procure and read feminist literature, such as Mary Wollstonecraft's *Vindication of the Rights of Women*.

The concept of separate spheres increased the discontent of ladies in two ways. First, many railed against the limitations imposed on them by the idea of women's proper roles. Second, as historian Nancy F. Cott has observed, woman's separate sphere caused a group consciousness to grow among women, which in turn led them to identify common problems and manifestations of oppression. The desire of some ladies to find ways to relieve their frustrations would eventually put them in the forefront of the feminist movement. In the meantime, however, most American women seemed to accept the equating of home, morality, and motherhood with women. Ladies, and even many mill girls and farm women, aspired to achieve some degree of "ladyhood" through the development of domestic and feminine virtues.

It may seem strange that the maxim "woman's place is in the home" received so much attention at a time when many women were actually leaving their homes for paid employment. Several scholars have argued that it was precisely because the traditional role of wife and mother was being challenged by industrial developments that Americans felt a pressing need to promote and protect it. One historian has suggested that women were given the home as their undisputed province in the hope that they would stay in it. Another has claimed that, by making women the protectors of virtue, men were free to engage in compromising business practices without fear of polluting their homes and families. But sociologist Carolyn E. Sachs believes that domestic ideology was related to industrialization because it encouraged increased consumption of factory goods by full-time homemakers while maintaining home-bound women as a reserve labor supply. She adds that the concept of women's domesticity also justified low wages and restricted opportunities for female workers whose "real" jobs were in their own homes.

Although the causes for the development of separate spheres for men and women are difficult to pinpoint, their effects are not hard to identify. Extensive changes resulted when large numbers of men moved their work away from the home to cities and factories, while large numbers of women were expected to remain within those homes. For instance, women were effectively cut out of family businesses, which were now formally organized and located some distance from the home. No longer could women learn trades and professions from fathers, brothers, and husbands. As a result, the number of women operating businesses declined compared to the colonial period. Those women who were involved in business usually served other women by supplying millinery, yard goods, or notions.

One exception was Sarah Todd Astor, a businesswoman of the day who did not engage in "feminine" business pursuits. She helped her husband Jacob parlay her dowry of $300 into a lucrative fur business, the American Fur Company. While he traveled to locate and trade furs, she managed the business, processed and graded furs, and gave birth to eight children in their home above the shop. Due to the investment of the profits of the American Fur Company in New York real estate, the Astor fortune was reputed to be the largest in the country at the time of Sarah's death in 1832.

Rebecca Pennock Lukens was another woman of the era who was involved in a male-dominated industry. On his deathbed, Lukens's husband asked her to take over the family iron mill in Pennsylvania. As a Quaker, she was well educated and had always been encouraged to take an interest in the family metalworking enterprise. After her husband's death, Lukens not only saved the mill from bankruptcy but added iron plate rolling to the business, supplying boilers for steamboats and locomotives. She was so successful that she was worth $100,000 at the time of her death in 1854. But, because her daughters were proper ladies who believed in domesticity, control of the Lukens Steel Company went to her sons-in-law instead of to them.

Astor and Lukens were unusual in that they refused to be segregated into feminine businesses. Most women were powerless to resist exclusion, especially from the professions of medicine and law. Because women were generally barred from medical and law schools and from serving internships with practicing physicians and attorneys, they could not hope to pass the licensing examinations that most states now required. By the 1820s, all but three states mandated licenses for medical practitioners. The examinations were based on techniques (such as the use of forceps) learned only in medical schools, so women were incapable of succeeding even if they had been permitted to take the tests.

On the other hand, women were increasingly granted access to the profession of teaching and nursing, which was just beginning to develop as an organized profession. Men were leaving these fields for jobs that paid more and offered continuous employment. Both teaching and nursing offered low pay, little status, and no security, but women rushed in to fill the void. These occupations seemed to be simply an extension of their home duties of teaching and caring for family members. In addition, most women could live with the drawbacks because they planned to marry and fulfill their domestic destinies rather than to fill these jobs for life. Consequently, teaching and nursing became classified as "women's work," with all the attendant disadvantages, such as low pay, because of women's willingness to accept the existing situation.

The development of separate spheres also affected family relationships. Among the lower classes, men, women, and children frequently went to the factory together each day. Yet, at night, women were expected to cook, wash, and care for the children. Such families often lived in the shantytowns, tenements, and slum districts of industrial cities. Disease and epidemics were rife, fire was a constant threat, and the crime rate was reputed to be the highest in the world. Given these dangerous conditions, how was a working woman to practice domesticity and establish an aura of morality in her overcrowded and shabby home? And how could she train and rear children who were already engaged in full-time factory labor by the age of seven or eight?

The life of ladies, of course, was very different. Their social class could not protect them entirely from disease, fire, or crime, but it could provide some amenities such as theaters, restaurants, and country clubs. Like their employed counterparts, ladies' husbands also left the home each day. But these women had many hours in which to complete their domestic tasks, and some had the help of servants as well.

Because household chores and overseeing servants consumed only a portion of their days, ladies sought out a variety of other activities. One of these focused on the need for ladies to dress lavishly in order to enhance their husbands' status. Ladies often became very concerned with their clothing, which was usually ornate and overdone. Ribbons, flowers, flounces, and ruffles bedecked almost every outfit. Intricate hats and bonnets were absolute necessities, as were gloves, a parasol, reticule (purse), and high-buttoned shoes. The outfits themselves contained as much as 100 yards of material and, in combination with whalebone stays and hoops, weighed fifteen to twenty pounds. When chemise, pantaloons, corset, corset cover, petticoats, and hoops were added, getting dressed was a one- to two-hour project in itself. Once dressed, poring over yards-goods samples, ribbons, or bonnet makings in a favorite shop could consume many more hours.

Ladies also paid considerable attention to their complexions, which they believed should be delicate and pale. They protected their hands and face from the sun and avoided the use of "paints" on their faces. Presumably, the lady demonstrated her leisure through a pallor that indicated little activity. Certainly she avoided exercise other than manuevering her hoopskirts into carriages and through doorways. Inactivity combined with tight corseting made the fainting couch a necessary piece of furniture for women who often felt weak and dizzy.

Ladies took great care with their decorum as well as their appearance. They avoided discussing politics and current events, speaking only of approved ladylike topics instead. They used proper language that indicated their modesty: "limb" for "leg" and "female" or "lady" for "woman." European visitors reported that some ladies were so modest that they even covered piano "limbs" with frilled trousers and draped nude statuary.

Filling their spare time could be a problem for these ladies. Most of them busied themselves with fancy needlework such as embroidery and craft work such as the making of hyacinth stands and glove boxes. Almost all of them played the piano, sang, studied French, and pursued other female "accomplishments." They read, but they were supposed to limit themselves to "morally improving" works of literature and poetry.

They also spent a good deal of time visiting with other women during the morning call or afternoon tea. In fact, many women formed close ties with other women. In 1834, author Catharine Sedgwick wrote that these strong, affectionate relationships between women were "nearest to the love of angels."

Wealthy women commonly spent few hours with their children, who were with nannies and tutors. When in their mother's company, boys were allowed to run and play certain games, but girls were expected to sit quietly sewing or reading. They saw their fathers briefly at dinner or bedtime, often in their role as major disciplinarians of the family. The closeness of the colonial American family was clearly unknown to these middle- and upperclass children.

The process of birthing continued to change as well. Male doctors increasingly dominated the delivery room. It became more common for the expectant mother's husband to be included, but whether he was there for emotional support or to police the behavior of the attending physician remains unclear. Perhaps the greatest related change during these years was women's growing demand for birth control information. Many forms of birth control such as abortions, douches, withdrawal, condoms, and devices to cover the cervix date back to ancient times. By the 1820s, women were not only asking about them but were apparently utilizing them; the birthrate dropped, particularly in urban areas.

At the same time, women were being told that their reproductive organs determined their physical health as well as their social roles. A malfunction of the uterus, thought to be linked to the entire nervous system, could cause backaches, headaches, insomnia, irritability, and a whole gamut of "nervous" disorders. Female ailments, as they were termed, supposedly determined a woman's emotions and achievements. Women's disorders were commonly treated through cauterizing the uterus, saline injections, and inserting leeches into the vagina. Not surprisingly, women rejected these practices in favor of such cures as diet reform, animal magnetism, and phrenology. They followed the preachings of health reformers who stressed exercise, fresh air, and the consumption of grains. And they sought out such unlicensed practitioners as Dr. Harriot Hunt, who, in Boston during the 1830s, pursued homeopathic, preventive medicine and studied the psychological bases of women's medical problems.

It seems evident that some serious contradictions existed between the dictates of the image of womanhood and its actual implementation. In reality: many women worked outside of the home; many ladies thought in terms of oppression and property rights rather than submissiveness; and many women attempted to exercise control over their bodies and reproduction instead of accepting "God's will" in such matters.

This discrepancy can be seen in other areas as well. In the arts, for example, women did continue to produce quilts, rugs, bed coverings, wall hangings, and other domestic artwork. The teachings of domesticity encouraged women to enhance their homes with their own artistic creations. One bit of advice assured women that "it is the province of woman to make the home. . . . " and that "If she makes that delightful and salutary—the abode of order and purity, though she may never herself step beyond the threshold—she may yet send forth from her humble dwelling, a power that will be felt round the globe." Consequently, many talented women used needle and thread instead of brush and paint and pieces of cloth instead of canvas.

But many women refused to accept the dogma by practicing the fine arts. They were always self-taught and were usually wives and mothers. One of the most notable of these was Eunice Pinney, who reared five children while becoming a prolific watercolor artist. Her vigorous and forthright work included landscapes, mourning pictures, and religious, historical, and literary scenes. Ruth Henshaw Bascom also combined domestic duties and art by "taking profiles" with pastel crayons.

Other women artists defied other domestic conventions. Mary Ann Willson lived openly with a Miss Brundage, whom she described as her "romantic attachment," and augmented their income by selling her paintings. Highly original and lively, these were done with paints made from berries, brick dust, and vegetable dyes. Deborah Goldsmith traveled alone from town to town plying her trade of limner, or portrait painter. Other itinerant portraitists were Susan Waters and S. A. Shute, who were much in demand by middle- and upperclass Americans who desired their likenesses preserved for posterity.

Such women artists challenged the words of commentators who warned them that "art is the most difficult—perhaps, in its highest form—almost impossible to women." Barred from enrolling in art schools and displaying in galleries, women did indeed have a difficult time learning to be artists. They were believed to have a "natural repugnance" to drawing from "life," or in other words, from nude models. Thus, according to one clergyman, "no virtuous and delicate female, who rightly appreciates the design of her being, and desires to sustain her own influence and that of her sex, and fulfill the high destiny for which she is formed, would desire to abate one jot or tittle from the seeming restrictions imposed upon her conduct."

Despite these stern words, many women did struggle against these limitations. A widespread desire to expand the female sphere erupted not only in art but in education as well. During these years, supporters of "improved female education" began to dispute the widely accepted idea that women's minds were smaller and weaker than men's, thus making women uneducable. In 1818, Hannah Mather Crocker, granddaughter of Cotton Mather, stated in *Observations on the Real Rights of Women:* "There can be no doubt but there is as much difference in the powers of each individual of the male sex as there is of the female: and if they receive the same mode of education, their improvement would be fully equal." Other proponents of women's education also argued that, if women were given "equal advantages" with men, they would soon prove that they were capable of being educated.

Critics responded that there was no reason for women to be educated since they were confined to a domestic vocation. What difference would it make if women's minds were equal to men's since they did not need to use them in the same ways? Reformers turned the principles of domesticity to their own ends when they answered that motherhood demanded education if its practice was to produce salutary adults. While they did not wish to see a woman "emulate the schoolmen's fame," they did believe that a woman's "mental and moral improvement" was necessary for her success as a mother and the happiness of her family. Their assertion that "men will never be wise while women are ignorant" was difficult to dispute.

In 1837, French commentator Auguste Carlier noted: "Ideas in America do not yet seem to be sufficiently settled in reference to the range of women's education. This is often superficial: at other times it embraces the Latin language, mathematics, trigonometry, algebra, etc." Reformers argued for academic subjects while traditionalists supported fashionable accomplishments. Those who emphasized the accomplishments realized that women were expected to attract husbands and then please them. Even the reformers recognized the economic and social importance of marriage to women. They cautioned young women to acquire knowledge with great modesty while "looking up" to the men on whom they depended.

Several women tried to resolve this ongoing debate by educating women in "serious" subjects. Emma Hart Willard upgraded her own Middlebury Seminary to show what women could do with such topics as algebra, trigonometry, history, and geography. In 1819, she appealed to the New York legislature for state aid for women's education. She had come to believe that female education could be equal only if it were publicly supported, as was men's. Not only was Willard's request refused, but a newspaper commented that "they will be educating the cows next." Willard refused to be discouraged and, in 1821, founded the Troy Female Seminary in New York, the first school in the United States to offer a high-school education to women.

A few years later, Scottish-born reformer Frances Wright publicly lectured on the need for public education for all Americans, including women. "Until women assume the place in society which good sense and good feeling alike assign to them," Wright reasoned, "human improvement must advance but feebly." She concluded that, "whenever men establish their own pretensions upon the sacrificed rights of others, we do in fact impeach our own liberties, and lower ourselves in the scale of being."

Advocates of women's education added another dimension to the discussion when they suggested that women needed better training in order to become teachers. Not only were women actually moving into teaching jobs, but a belief in their special qualities as teachers was growing. Supporters of women as teachers emphasized women's innately high character, capacity for affection that would make students anxious to respond to them, and maternal instincts that would allow them to build a greater familiarity and rapport than would be proper for the "other sex."

Other supporters of teacher training for women emphasized the low cost of women teachers. By the 1850s, in an appeal to Congress for appropriations for women's teacher training programs, Catharine Beecher pointed out that "Women can afford to teach for one-half, or even less, the salary which men would ask, because the female teacher has only to sustain herself; she does not look forward to the duty of supporting a family, should she marry, nor has she the ambition to amass a fortune." The argument for women teachers as highly moral and cost-effective may have opened doors for them, but it also created damaging stereotypes that would have to be confronted by later generations.

Women's growing assertiveness led them to work to expand not only their educations but their religious participation. The Second Great Awakening was characterized by female evangelism. Women fostered and organized revivals and directed a militant piety against ungodly and unchurched men. During the Second Great Awakening, women converts outnumbered men by three to two. Women were also prominent in the revival movement in western New York. By 1814, women dominated the churches and religious societies of Utica. According to historian Barbara L. Epstein, women protested against male authority through the acceptable forum of religious zeal. While staying within the bounds of feminine behavior, religious women forced their wills on men by pushing them toward religious activity.

Women also dominated the Sunday schools that were beginning to appear in many churches. By claiming that their inherent virtue qualified them, rather than men, to instruct children in religious values, women essentially seized positions of power within their congregations. Their roles as Sunday-school teachers effectively allowed women to ignore the Pauline doctrine regarding women's silence in church. Through their devoted and selfless commitment to religion, such women created a new and more serious view of women for themselves, their students, and their associates. Their establishment of the image of evangelical womanhood provided both a challenge and an alternative to the frivolous aspect of ladyhood.

As women became the majority of congregants, the clergy responded to their increasing religious participation by continuing to feminize their teachings. For example, in response to mothers' protests against the harsh doctrine of infant damnation due to innate human sin, ministers began to agree that good Christian nurturing could offset original sin. Ministers also supported the concept of superior female morality. They confirmed the growing belief that women exceeded men in piety and purity. In an 1810 sermon, one preacher exclaimed, "We look to you, ladies, to raise the standard of character in our own sex."

In historian Barbara Welter's view, the result of the growing feminization of religion was an emphasis on introspection and morality. Women learned to assess their characters and believe in their strengths—two abilities that propelled them toward independence rather than toward domesticity. The stress that religion placed on brotherhood and equality of men before God became, for many women, a sense of sisterhood and equality of women before God. Women's growing commitment to religious activity was thus at once a protest against their restricted roles and an active attack upon them. Clearly, both the prescription and the practice of American womanhood were complex matters during this era. They proved confusing to white American women. They provided a challenge in adaptation to immigrant women. And they totally bypassed black and American Indian women.

Most black women found their roles and lifestyles dictated by the slave system. They had little control over their domesticity, child-care practices, or even the moral climate in which they lived. They were compelled to perform heavy labor, provide sexual services to white men, and give up the care of their children to women too elderly to work in the fields. Although marriage was an important institution for slave women, it often proved to be unstable through no fault of their own. As one black minister noted, slaves married "until death or distance do you part," a situation that created highly independent wives and mothers who could not count on the presence and aid of men. Black women, who bore an average of four to five children, were also frequently denied the satisfaction of raising their offspring. Mother-child bonds were strong and probably accounted for the fact that less slave women ran away then men. As a result of the instability of the black family under slavery, black women devoted much of their energy to maintaining kinship ties and to creating new kinship networks when slavery destroyed old ones.

Slave women were also laborers outside of their homes. On plantations and farms, black women worked in a wide variety of taxing and often skilled jobs, including those of domestic servants, washwomen, nursemaids, field hands, and artisans. According to one slave woman, women's work was often difficult to distinguish from men's:

> Over there, you would see a road all turned up and you would see men and women both throwing up dirt and rocks; the men would haul it off and the women would take picks and things and get it up. You could any day see a woman, a whole lot of 'em making a road. Could look up and see ten women up over dar on the hill plowing and look over the other way and see ten more. I have done everything on a farm what a man done 'cept cut wheat. I split rails like a man. I used a iron wedge drove into the wood with a maul. I drive the gin, what was run by two mules.

In southern industry, black women worked as heavy labor in cotton and woolen mills, turpentine camps, sugar refineries, food and tobacco factories, hemp manufactories, foundries, saltworks, and mines. They also worked as lumberjacks and ditchdiggers, helping to build levees and lay track for southern railroads. Slave women also worked in southern cities as chambermaids, nursemaids, hairdressers, seamstresses, domestic servants, and vendors.

Yet, in spite of their large economic contributions to the development of the southern economy, black slave women were generally denied pay or other recognition of their labor and were seldom granted any privileges. Slave women faced gender-related difficulties that black men did not. Because the demand for slaves overwhelmed the supply of them after the end of the slave trade in 1809, black women were expected to reproduce as frequently as possible. As one slave woman noted, the more children she had, the more she was worth. Some black women were confined to breeding farms, other "breeders" and "fancy girls" brought prices and were well cared for, while others were expected to continue with their usual tasks while pregnant. In addition, women were not released from domestic tasks or the care of their own families because they labored in the fields. Rather, they were subject to such double burdens as tending cotton while nursing their babies in the fields.

In the "big house" black slave women labored heavily for long hours. Subject to constant surveillance and punishment, they were cut off from their families and friends for many hours of each day. They were also subject to sexual coercion by the white masters with whom they were in constant contact. At the same time, they had to bear the callous treatment of white mistresses who resented their husband's sexual activities. And when children were the product of such unions, slave women were denied the time and resources to care for them properly. Black women subtly rebelled against economic and sexual exploitation by avoiding sexual relationships with both white and black men, aborting unwanted fetuses, and even committing infanticide to save a child from the horrors of the slave system.

Even the slave women who were allowed to practice such skills as nursing, healing, and midwifery for pay seldom derived any benefit from it. One slave woman who was trained as a midwife at the age of thirteen earned substantial sums of money for her owner. In her words:

> I made a lot o' money for old miss. Lots of times, didn't get sleep regular or git my meals on time for three-four days. Cause when dey call, I always went. Brought as many white as culled children. I's brought lots of 'em an' I ain't never lost a case.

In addition to their many other burdens, slave women were expected to care for their families and homes as best they could. Resentful of slave owners' tendency to ignore gender when making assignments to field labor, slave women often sought to preserve their sense of being women by establishing a strict division of labor within their homes. They typically performed most housekeeping tasks and child-care chores themselves despite the heavy demands on their energies by other duties outside of their homes. Thus, slave women were not only involved in the production of goods and services, but they produced and cared for future workers under extremely taxing conditions. They resisted this system that destroyed their families and ignored their gender by attempting to maintain their homes with pride and to tend their families with care. Moreover, they clung to native customs and attempted to instill a respect for their race in their children.

Free black women were only slightly better off. A study of free black women in Petersburg, Virginia, indicates that they held jobs and headed households. Free black women could also, at least theoretically, protest against injustice and use the courts. They formed organizations, published newspapers and books, and joined abolitionist societies. Better than one hundred works of fiction, protest, and autobiography were written by former slaves and free blacks between 1810 and 1860.

Yet free black women were exploited, underpaid, and denied opportunities for education or advancement. The jobs that they held were often exhausting and low-paying, and the households they headed were often not formed by their own choice. In northern cities, free black women, forced by economic necessity to seek employment primarily as domestic servants, were hired by white women who believed them to be docile and passive. White employees required black domestics to live in and treated them much like surrogate slaves. Other black women sewed, or took in laundry, often for the fee of about one cent per shirt. Still others engaged in hairdressing, flower selling, hat cleaning, or other services. Northern mines and factories generally did not hire free black women. Adhering to racist stereotypes of black women as "lazy" and "morally corrupt," white employers and workers refused to accept black women as factory operatives. Other free black women were not able to find jobs at all. In 1827, a black newspaper, *Freedom's Journal,* stated that there were forty-three black women paupers in New York City alone.

Like their slave counterparts, free black women worked diligently to establish meaningful values and activities. Some attempted to improve their educations by forming groups like the "Afric-American Female Intelligence Society" of Boston in 1832. Other free black women, such as Sarah Mapps Douglass of Philadelphia, became teachers themselves. In 1820, Douglass opened a school for free black children and actively participated in the Philadelphia Female Anti-slavery Society, of which she was a founding member. Yet, in 1837, Douglass heatedly described her segregation to a back bench designated for "the people of color" in a Quaker meetinghouse. She concluded that, while some Friends had cleansed themselves "of the foul stain of prejudice," the majority despised her people "for our color."

In a sense, free black women were pathbreakers. They earned wages and even maintained economic independence. Paradoxically, black women were able to work because it was widely understood that black female labor was the cheapest on the market. As women and as blacks, they could now be exploited as "wage slaves."

American Indian women were certainly no better off. With the white population doubling every twenty-five years, it was obvious that Indians would soon be outnumbered and overrun. Thomas Jefferson's prediction that native peoples could live in peace west of the Mississippi River for many years was not to materialize. Instead, white settlers swept across the Ohio and lower Mississippi valleys and began to cross the Mississippi River. They pushed American Indians along ahead of them, frequently destroying them in their haste and determination to settle the West.

As whites invaded native lands, they continued to take advantage of Indian women as guides, sexual partners, and domestic servants. They freely borrowed agricultural tools and methods from native women, but never acknowledged these women's ingenuity and expertise. Whites tended to ignore customary divisions of labor and the traditional crafts of Indian peoples. For example, during the 1830s, the United States Commissioner of Indian Affairs classified the Cherokee as a hunting society because the men hunted. This view totally overlooked the fact that Cherokee women had been adept and productive agriculturalists for centuries. It seemed impossible for white eyes to see women's work as significant, if not crucial. Instead, the Commissioner's office declared that Cherokee women must be taught to spin and weave while the men must be taught to farm. Not only did this prescription slight women's crafts, but it forced men into taking over the growing of crops, long considered to be uniquely within women's realm.

Euro-Americans usually recognized only those native women who helped them to achieve their own objectives. As a case in point, Milly Francis, a Creek Indian woman, received a congressional medal and a small pension for saving a white captive from death at the hands of her people in 1817. By now, it was evident that American Indian women could expect little from white Americans except more pain and exploitation.

Such treatment was extended to Mexican women as well. As whites poured into Texas during the 1830s, they often reacted in a biased fashion to the Mexicans whom they encountered. With heads filled with a negative picture of Mexican character derived from articles, reports, and letters, white settlers leveled harsh criticism against Mexicans. Although the stereotypes were vastly overdrawn, they were indicative of the nativist and racial prejudices of the day. In 1831, one female visitor to Texas wrote that Mexicans were, "generally speaking, timid and irresolute" and also "brutal" and "cowardly." She claimed that even the Comanche Indians liked Americans better than they did Mexicans.

These cruel characterizations of Mexicans seemed to overlook the fact that American settlers were guests in Mexican territory, and as such, it was perhaps less than gracious to so harshly criticize their hosts. In years to come, American disdain for Mexicans would increase, and a growing spirit of Manifest Destiny would convince Americans of their right to add Texas to the Union in 1845, California and environs in 1848, and the Gadsden Purchase in 1853. Although the Mexican frontier would thus become part of the American frontier, assimilation and intermarriage proceeded slowly. The view of Mexicans held by Euro-Americans stood as a barrier between the two groups for many decades.

The westward movement was a much more pleasant experience for white female settlers than it was for the people they displaced. Many women found attractive reasons for relocating to frontier regions that extended to the Mississippi River and beyond by the 1820s. Although their menfolk often made the actual decision, women could appreciate the chance of restored health for a family member in a more favorable climate, the opportunity to recoup a financial disaster sustained by the family, a fortune to be gained from the utilization of natural resources, or the potential of a prosperous future on cheap, available farm land. European women looked toward the American West as a place where they could enjoy landownership, practice religious toleration, or escape tyrannical governments. Army wives chose to follow their husbands to frontier forts. Religious orders of women relocated in the West to serve and educate native peoples. Single women chose to migrate in order to find husbands, procure employment, take up land, or serve as missionaries and teachers.

For many reasons, then, women began the westward trek with husbands, families, and friends in conveyances that ranged from stagecoaches and railroad cars to the legendary Conestoga wagon. Wagons, either the smaller emigrant wagon or the larger prairie schooner, were popular because they contained abundant space for people and possessions. When selected, the wagon was outfitted for the journey. Men equipped it with running gear, trained the horses or oxen that would pull it, and prepared tools, firearms, and stock. Women stitched the wagon cover and readied food, clothing, bedding, and medicines.

While these arrangements progressed, people began to prepare themselves for the coming traumatic separation from the friends and family with whom they had spent their lives. After tearful and often prolonged partings, the migrants were on their way. Once on the trail, they were hardly isolated. Their journals tell of meeting old friends and neighbors and of making new friends. Women visited with other women and exchanged recipes and bits of useful trail lore. One woman's diary contained frequent references to storytelling, music, songs, laughter, and merrymaking.

Although loneliness was not part of the trail routine for women, hard work was. Daily living had to continue despite the trail environment. Women cooked meals over campfires, laid beds out under the stars, and washed clothing in streams. Older children aided women in these tasks, and men sometimes set up tables, started fires, and even cooked. Still, women's chores were extremely heavy. Because of trail conditions, women's work became more intricate and more wearying than it had been before departure. In addition, many trail women were pregnant or nursing infants, which further complicated their numerous trail duties.

Yet women's complaints were not overwhelming. Many women prided themselves on their "housekeeping." Kitturah Belknap, on her way to Iowa in the 1830s, took "good earthen dishes" backed up with tinware and "four nice little table cloths" that she made. She supplemented her family's food by buying fresh produce from farms, baking bread that she set to rise on the warm ground under the wagon during the night, and producing rolls of butter by letting the motion of the lurching wagon operate the churn inside it.

The westward trek was arduous for women. The weather was often frightful, wagons broke down, oxen died, and people fell ill and died. Women were expected to help with men's work, such as driving the wagon or herding stock, at the same time that they tried to protect their children from trail accidents. Some women naturally grew discouraged and turned back. As one explained it: "Some liked the new country, but others returned to their native States."

Most women, however, hung on. They recognized that their efforts were crucial to the success of the migration. Any domestic routines that they would establish, any help that they could offer, any support that they could give were all hedges against the disintegration of the undertaking. In addition, these were farm women who were familiar with most of the tasks that were demanded of them. They approached the trail experience as a time of transition, during which they could hone their skills and prepare their minds for what lay ahead. As one said; "I never thought about its being hard. I was used to things being hard."

When women arrived in their new regions, their reactions were mixed. One recalled that, "when we got to the new purchase, the land of milk and honey, we were disappointed and homesick, but we were there and had to make the best of it." Others remembered being dismayed by native peoples, cold winters, wet springs, hot summers, mosquitoes, and "wild beasts." One woman pragmatically wrote to her mother: "I can't say I like the West as well as I do New England yet I think it is better for me to be here." At the same time, many women were ecstatic at the sight of prairie flowers, green rolling valleys, and flowing rivers. One young woman claimed not to be disillusioned even when she saw the primitive log cabin that was her new home. In "girl fashion," she explained, "I considered it very romantic."

Most women were not so pleased with their first homes, which were anything from the wagon that carried them westward to a corncrib, an abandoned outbuilding, lean-to, tarpaper shack, sod hut, or log cabin. But, despite its condition, women turned their energies to converting their first shelters into homes for their families and workplaces for themselves. Women often complained of frost on the walls, snowflakes on the blankets and table, and ice on the floors. In some regions, wind was the major problem because it carried dust into clothing, cooking utensils, and food. Scorching sun, torrential rains, bugs, and snakes were other enemies of frontier housekeepers. Women endured them all because they realized that their early homes represented the youth of the frontier and marked a stage that every raw frontier community had to tolerate. So they hung quilts as room dividers, papered the walls with newspapers or painted them with lime, and created household furnishings out of packing crates and rope.

With her workplace established, the frontierswoman turned her energies to producing candles, soap, clothing, foodstuffs, and a wide variety of other domestic goods. All of these products demanded ingenuity, expertise, and incredible amounts of time. In addition, women bore many children, educated them, and trained them as domestic or field laborers. They were also expert herbalists who served as apothecaries and morticians to their families and friends. And they brought in all the cash that their families would ever see through the sales of their butter, eggs, knitted goods, and other products.

Despite the fact that these women functioned in their homes as domestic artisans who converted the raw produce of the fields into finished goods, the United States census of the 1830s listed these women as "not gainfully employed." In this industrial economy, only those people who actually received paychecks were considered to be "employed," yet it is impossible to dispute the tremendous significance of women's labor to the frontier economy.

Most frontierswomen found that the worst was over in about two years. They moved into better homes, could buy many items from stores in the new towns that were rapidly springing up, and had friends and neighbors to relieve the initial loneliness. Churches and schools appeared, which gave them other social outlets.

Women were also relieved of field labor as soon as the homestead was established. Sachs has argued that American farm women rejected field work as a means of resisting direction from men. By limiting themselves to the home and garden, women freed themselves of supervision and control. Men retained their authority outside of the home as a result. Thus, the frontier, contrary to popular belief, did not break down the usual division of labor along gender lines. Rather, frontierswomen worked to perpetuate the same labor system within the family that they had always known.

Women also attempted to reestablish domesticity and other feminine values in their new homes. For example, they continued to wear hoop skirts and follow the fashion plates in *Godey's Lady's Book*. They wore sunbonnets to protect their faces from the sun. And they decorated their homes with craftwork and folk art, particularly exquisite quilts that often told a story or recorded family history. For instance, Elizabeth Mitchell of Kentucky used her Coffin Quilt to note family deaths by taking labeled coffins from the quilt's border and moving them into the graveyard in its center.

At the same time, frontierswomen also resisted the dictates of domesticity. They sought education in the country schoolhouses and early women's seminaries. In most regions, coeducation was an accepted practice from the beginning of settlement. Women also rapidly moved into teaching so that most western areas had a higher proportion of female teachers than did eastern states. Women also took up paid employment as railway station agents, team drivers, shepherds, store clerks, prostitutes, lawyers, musicians, artists, authors, journalists, and a wide variety of other jobs. They sometimes voted in local elections and discussed issues such as equality, landownership, and the right of suffrage. In fact, American women would eventually be first granted the vote in several western territories and states.

Until just a few years ago, available information on frontiersmen was vast and varied while that on frontierswomen was sparse and stereotyped. As miner, cowboy, soldier, sodbuster, rancher, or outlaw, the frontiersman captured people's imaginations. On the infrequent occasions when the frontierswoman happened to receive some attention, it was also in romanticized terms. Over the years, frontierswomen have been portrayed as Gentle Tamers, Pioneers in Petticoats, Saints in Sunbonnets, Madonnas of the Prairie, Pioneer Mothers, Light Ladies, Calamity Janes, and Fighting Feminists. On the one hand, the frontierswoman was admired for her tenacity. On the other, she was pitied for her sad fate. At one time, sympathy was expressed for her intrinsic weakness and the domesticity of nature that limited her potential for success on the frontier. At another time, she was commended for her bravery, courage, and fortitude.

What was the reality of frontierswomen? Were they gaunt, pathetic figures in faded calico dresses and tattered sunbonnets? Did they cry and beg to return to their former homes? Or did they bravely face the sun and, with a small child in one hand and a rifle in the other, help to conquer the American West? The truth lies somewhere between the extremes. Some frontierswomen were gaunt, pathetic, and ragged, but others were healthy, hardy, and well-dressed. Some women did hate to leave their homes, but others initiated the idea or migrated on their own. Most of those who stayed on the frontier made incalculable contributions to the settlement of the American West.

Frontierwomen did not display any single characteristic. They exhibited a full spectrum of personalities, talents, abilities, and attitudes. They came from a variety of backgrounds. They followed a large number of careers ranging from homemaker to field hand. In other words, their lives were so multifaceted that they cannot be explained by an image or a stereotype. As one woman said of the fabled sunbonnet, "they were an obstruction to sight and an impediment to hearing." And so it has been with the mystique surrounding the women who wore the sunbonnets. Fortunately, the reality of their lives, roles, and participation in the development of the frontier is finally emerging from its shroud.

Of course, it must be remembered that in reality all American women's lives during the years between 1816 and 1837 were complicated, frequently perplexing, and often full of ambiguity. Many views of women emerged during this era from observers, commentators, and historians who all viewed women through the filter of their own perceptions. For example, in 1835, the writings of a French visitor, Alexis de Tocqueville, presented American women as protected, elevated, and superior beings. To him, the American family was like a miniature democracy, with the man as its head and the woman and children as its citizens. De Tocqueville insisted that, "although the women of the United States are confined within the narrow circle of domestic life, and their situation is in some respects one of extreme dependence, I have nowhere seen woman occupying a loftier position."

Only two years later, another European traveler presented an opposing assessment of American women. According to English writer Harriet

Martineau, women's intellects were confined, their morals crushed, health ruined, weakness encouraged, and strength punished. She condemned public chivalry as an "indulgence" given to women "as a substitute for justice." Marriage was to her "a poor institution" in which "one sex overbears the other." She lamented the shameful treatment of female workers and black slave women. In Martineau's eyes, "the Americans have, in their treatment of women, fallen below, not only their own democratic principles, but the practice of some parts of the Old World." Because America did not extend the principles of the Declaration of Independence to all of its citizens, Martineau found it a disappointing and hypocritical country.

Did the majority of American women fit De Tocqueville's or Martineau's description? Did they see the system in which they lived as beneficent or degrading? Did they adhere to the model of True Womanhood as closely as possible or subvert it at every opportunity? Had the Industrial Revolution and the westward movement brought progress or setback to the images and realities of their lives? All of these questions are clearly impossible to answer with any assurance.

It is clear, however, that numerous women were beginning to exert their talents and time to modify both American society and the model of True Womanhood. Apparently dissatisfied with many of the changes that had occurred in America during the Industrial Revolution, these women were in the forefront of what was soon to become a national reform movement. When the nation's worst economic crisis to date, the Panic of 1837, temporarily interrupted industrialization, the nation was already turning its attention to restructuring a society fraught with problems. Women enthusiastically originated and participated in the increasing numbers and types of reform activities. What remains to be seen is how these women divided their energies between reshaping American life in general and redefining the model of womanhood in particular to stretch the limits of the female "sphere."

SUGGESTIONS FOR FURTHER READING

Boylan, Anne M. "Evangelical Womanhood in the Nineteenth Century: The Role of Women in Sunday Schools." *Feminist Studies* 4 (October 1978): 62–80.

Brownlee, W. Elliot. "Household Values, Women's Work, and Economic Growth, 1800-1923." *Journal of Economic History* 39 (March 1979): 199–209.

Clinton, Catherine. *The Plantation Mistress: Woman's World in the Old South.* New York: Pantheon Books, 1980.

——. *The Other Civil War: American Women in the Nineteenth Century.* New York: Hill and Wang, 1984. Chapter 2.

Cott, Nancy F. *The Bonds of Womanhood: "Woman's Sphere" In New England, 1780–1835.* New Haven: Yale University Press, 1977.

Dewhurst, C. Kurt, Betty MacDowell, and Marsha MacDowell. *Artists in Aprons: Folk Art by American Women*. New York: E. P. Dutton, 1979.

Dublin, Thomas. *Women at Work: The Transformation of Work and Community in Lowell, Massachusetts, 1826–1860*. New York: Columbia University Press, 1979.

———. *Farm to Factory: The Mill Experience and Women's Lives in New England, 1830–1860*. New York: Columbia University Press, 1981.

Dudden, Faye E. *Serving Women: Household Service in Nineteenth-Century America*. Middletown, CT: Wesleyan University Press, 1983.

Dysart, Jane. "Mexican Women in San Antonio, 1830–1860: The Assimilation Process." *Western Historical Quarterly* 7 (October 1976): 365–375.

Ellison, Mary. "Resistance to Oppression: Black Women's Response to Slavery in the United States." *Slavery and Abolition* 4 (May 1983): 56–63.

Epstein, Barbara Leslie. *The Politics of Domesticity: Women, Evangelism, and Temperance in Nineteenth-Century America*. Middletown, CT: Wesleyan University Press, 1981.

Gordon, Jean. "Early American Women Artists and the Social Context in Which They Worked." *American Quarterly* 30 (Spring 1978): 54–69.

Gordon, Linda. "The Long Struggle for Reproductive Rights." *Radical America* 15 (Spring 1981): 74–88.

Gutman, Herbert G. *The Black Family in Slavery and Freedom, 1750–1925*. New York: Pantheon Books, 1976.

Hagler, D. Harland. "The Ideal Woman in the Antebellum South: Lady or Farmwife?" *Journal of Southern History* XLV (August 1980): 405–418.

Harley, Sharon. "Northern Black Female Workers: Jacksonian Era." In *The Afro-American Woman: Struggles and Images*, edited by Sharon Harley and Rosalyn Terborg-Penn, 5–16. Port Washington, NY: Kennikat Press, 1978.

Hine, Darlene. "Female Slave Resistance: The Economics of Sex." *Western Journal of Black Studies* 3 (Summer 1979): 123–127.

James, Edward T., ed. *Notable American Women, 1607–1950: A Biographical Dictionary*. Cambridge, MA: Belknap Press, 1971.

Jensen, Joan M., and Darlis A. Miller. "The Gentle Tamers Revisited: New Approaches to the History of Women in the American West." *Pacific Historical Review* 49 (May 1980): 173–214.

Jensen, Joan M., and Sue Davidson, eds. *A Needle, a Bobbin, a Strike: Women Needleworkers in America*. Philadelphia: Temple University Press, 1984.

Jones, Jacqueline. "'My Mother Was Much of a Woman': Black Women, Work, and the Family Under Slavery." *Feminist Studies* 8 (Summer 1982): 235–269.

Kaufman, Polly Welts. *Women Teachers on the Frontier*. New Haven: Yale University Press, 1984.

Kessler-Harris, Alice. *Out to Work: A History of Wage-Earning Women in the United States*. New York: Oxford University Press, 1982.

Lebsock, Suzanne. "Free Black Women and the Question of Matriarchy: Petersburg, Virginia, 1784–1820." *Feminist Studies* 8 (Summer 1982): 270–292.

———. *The Free Women of Petersburg: Status and Culture in a Southern Town, 1784–1860*. New York: W. W. Norton & Co., Inc., 1983.

Lecompte, Janet. "The Independent Women of Hispanic New Mexico, 1821–1846." *Western Historical Quarterly* 12 (January 1981): 17–35.

Lerner, Gerda. "The Lady and the Mill Girl: Changes in the Status of Women in the Age of Jackson." *American Studies* 10 (Spring 1969): 5–15.

———. ed. *Black Women in White America: A Documentary History.* New York: Vintage Books, 1973.

Matthews, Jane D. "'Woman's Place' and the Search for Identity in Antebellum America." *The Canadian Review of American Studies* 10 (Winter 1979): 289–304.

Melder, Keith. "Women in the Shoe Industry: The Evidence from Lynn." *Essex Institute Historical Collections* 115 (October 1979): 270–287.

Miller, Darlis. "Cross-Cultural Marriages in the Southwest: The New Mexico Experience, 1846–1900." *New Mexico Historical Review* 57 (October 1982): 335–360.

Myres, Sandra L. *Westering Women and The Frontier Experience, 1800–1915.* Albuquerque: University of New Mexico Press, 1982.

———. "Mexican Americans and Westering Anglos: A Feminine Perspective." *New Mexico Historical Review* 57 (October 1982): 317–333.

Riley, Glenda. "Women in the West." *Journal of American Culture* 3 (Summer 1980): 311–329.

———. "'Not Gainfully Employed': Women on the Iowa Frontier, 1833–1870." *Pacific Historical Review* 49 (May 1980): 237–264.

———. *Frontierswomen: The Iowa Experience.* Ames: Iowa State University Press, 1981.

———, ed. *Women in the West.* Manhattan, KS: Sunflower University Press, 1982.

Ryan, Mary P. *Womanhood in America: From Colonial Times to the Present.* New York: New Viewpoints, 1979, Chapters 2 and 3.

Sachs, Carolyn E. *The Invisible Farmers: Women in Agricultural Production.* Totowa, NJ: Rowman and Allanheld, 1983.

Sterling, Dorothy. *We Are Your Sisters: Black Women in the Nineteenth-Century.* New York: W. W. Norton & Co., Inc., 1984.

Suitor, J. Jill. "Husbands' Participation in Childbirth: A Nineteenth-Century Phenomenon." *Journal of Family History* 6 (Fall 1981): 278–293.

Van de Wetering, Maxine. "The Popular Concept of 'Home' in Nineteenth-Century America." *Journal of American Studies* 18 (April 1984): 5–28.

Welter, Barbara. *Dimity Convictions: The American Woman in the Nineteenth Century.* Athens, OH: Ohio University Press, 1976.

When Sarah Josepha Hale became the editor of Godey's Lady's Book *in 1837, she attempted to enlarge the concepts of domesticity, woman's sphere, and women's moral guardianship of the home to include a variety of endeavors and interests not customarily associated with women's roles.* From Godey's Lady's Book, Philadelphia, Pennsylvania.

CHAPTER 4

Reshaping American Life and Values:
The Reform Era
1837–1861

B ETWEEN 1837 and 1861, the peak of the reform era, many women
were deeply involved in the national crusade to reshape and improve American life and institutions. In the course of their activities, they also changed the model of the American woman. When many
female reformers came to believe that it was necessary to crusade directly
for modifications in the status of women, the first American feminist
movement was born. As a result, the traditional image of womanhood
experienced the first overt onslaught on its form and influence since the
founding of the American colonies in 1607. Although it survived, its
foundations were definitely shaken and the stage set for future attacks.

Women's widespread efforts to enlarge their lives are illustrated in the
careers of many specific women who pursued a wide variety of approaches and arguments. One of these was editor and writer Sarah Josepha Hale, who dedicated her talents to reshaping American ways of
thinking regarding women. In 1836, Hale left Boston to become the editor of *Godey's Lady's Magazine*. Since her husband's death in 1823, Hale
had built a sound reputation as a poet, novelist, and editor dedicated to
the cause of "female improvement." In the first issue of her *Ladies' Magazine* in 1828, she assured her male readers that her purpose was to
encourage women to become more competent in their domestic duties
and more agreeable as companions. She intended to achieve these ends
by working for the improvement of "female education," which, in turn,
would increase women's effectiveness as the moral and purifying forces
of America. This approach proved to be appealing to both female and
male readers. As a result, her competitor, Louis Godey, bought Hale's
Ladies' Magazine and persuaded her to join him in Philadelphia.

As editor of *Godey's,* Hale became one of the primary proponents of
the concepts of women's sphere and the moral powers of women. In her

first issue in January 1837, she explained that the mission of *Godey's* was to "carry onward and upward the spirit of moral and intellectual excellence in our own sex, till their influence shall bless as well as beautify civil society. These principles we shall guard with scrupulous care, and watch that nothing be introduced to undermine those sacred relations of domestic life, in which the Creator has placed the sceptre of woman's empire." She followed this statement with a plethora of copy defining and developing her ideas regarding the improvement of women's status within their sphere. Throughout the 1830s, 1840s, and 1850s, Hale employed argument, exhortation, poetry, moral romance, and a variety of other techniques to achieve her objective.

The theme that ran throughout Hale's editorship of *Godey's* was that women were the moral guardians of society. While men engaged in necessary, and often compromising, business practices and public affairs, women served as the moral keepers of home and family. In 1847, Hale expressed this division of function in verse: "He must work—the world subduing/Till it blooms like Eden bright/She must watch—his faith renewing/From her urn of Eden light." Yet, while Hale maintained that women's place was in the home, she also promoted the expansion of the female sphere through improved education, simplified clothing styles that would allow increased activity, and women as teachers, authors of "moral" literature and poetry, missionaries, and medical practitioners. Hale's approach to widening women's sphere was so nonthreatening that she was revered and loved by generations of American readers of all ages.

Of course, Hale did not stand alone in promoting such thinking about women. Many other editors and authors contributed their interpretations and perspectives to the emerging model of the moral American woman. Legions of women writers wrote books that became immediate bestsellers during the 1830s, 1840s, and 1850s, but have languished on library shelves ever since. Domestic novels, as they were called because of their homey themes, frequently went through multiple and worldwide editions. These authors far outsold writers like Herman Melville and Nathaniel Hawthorne. In fact, Hawthorne was reportedly so disgusted with their success that he referred to them as that "damned mob of scribbling women."

One of the most eminent of these women writers was Harriet Beecher Stowe. Coming from a family of reformers and deeply interested in social reform herself, Stowe directed her early writings toward the issues of temperance, higher wages for seamstresses, and improved educational opportunities for women. Hale encouraged Stowe, and thus many of Stowe's first stories appeared in *Godey's*. She later became involved in the abolitionist movement and wrote several novels. In 1852, she became the most visible female author with *Uncle Tom's Cabin*.

Another domestic novelist of the period was Caroline Lee Hentz. She, too, published her occasional first stories in *Godey's* during the 1830s, but because of her husband's lack of business acumen, turned to writing fulltime to support her family. By the 1850s, Hentz was well-known for such novels as *Ernest Linwood* (1856). While she seemed to uphold all the usual ideals of women's moral powers and domestic sphere, the underlying theme of Hentz's work was what one commentator termed "mutilation of the male." Hentz's male characters were typically ill, imbecilic, or morally crippled, while her female protagonists were strong, decisive, all-suffering, and highly moral. A contemporary of Hentz, E. D. E. N. Southworth, removed males from the scene entirely. In such novels as *The Deserted Wife* (1851) and *The Discarded Daughter* (1852), Hentz sent men off to war, the West, or in pursuit of a pretty young woman. The women whom they left behind were self-dependent, energetic, and capable of supporting themselves and their children or siblings, often achieving fame and fortune in the process. When the abject husband returned, he was always forgiven by his magnanimous wife or daughter. That men could not function without the strength and morality of women was clearly the overriding message of both Hentz and Southworth.

A less vitriolic writer was Lydia B. Sigourney, known as "the Sweet Singer of Hartford." She, too, was forced by economic necessity to follow a literary career, which lasted over half a century and produced over fifty works. Her name became a byword for a generation of readers who fed upon the romanticized, didactic poems and stories that she began to produce in the mid-1830s. Like the other domestic writers, Sigourney lauded the traditional virtues of home and family in such works as *Whispers to a Bride* (1850) and *The Daily Counsellor* (1859) while flouting them in her own career and by subtleties in her writings. Eliza Leslie and Catherine M. Sedgwick, neither of whom ever married, also gained popularity by idealizing domesticity, although they rejected it in their own lives. Leslie's works, such as *Mr. and Mrs. Woodbridge and Other Tales* (1841), reiterated homely and wifely virtues, but Sedgwick, particularly in *Married or Single?* (1857), was an outspoken champion of the unmarried woman.

Elizabeth Fries Lummis Ellet took yet another approach to women's roles. She was interested in reconstructing the history of women to demonstrate that women had been prominent nurturers and guardians of American democracy. She also argued that women fulfilled a variety of social functions, did jobs considered to be "men's work," and contributed significantly to the settlement of the frontier. Her best known work, *The Women of the American Revolution*, which appeared in two volumes in 1848, was in its fourth edition by 1850.

Perhaps these women writers were so popular because they were not avowed reformers or feminists. At least on the surface, they preached all of the accepted views regarding women and did not deprecate the customary view of the family and women's place. They supported a perception of women that emphasized their moral guardianship of home and family. Yet, at the same time, these writers presented women as active, influential people. A study of almost two hundred domestic novels, short stories, and essays shows that these writers imparted a contradictory message. Their portrayals of domesticity were riddled with deep discontent. They characterized men as sinful, obsessed with a desire for wealth and social position, and in need of reform. Women were superior beings, responsible for their families and increasingly for guarding against the evils that existed in society as well.

This assignment of influence to women had wide implications. As moral keepers of society, women could conceivably undertake numerous endeavors. For example, the moral guardian theory justified the following positions: mothers must have education to mold their children correctly; women must write "morally improving" novels; women must understand politics to influence male legislators wisely; women must teach school to inculcate children with virtue; and women must form charity organizations to aid the poor and destitute. In short, morally superior women should dominate any function or social situation that would benefit from morality.

The possibilities of the moral guardian theory were almost unlimited. This theory in essence made it easier for women to stay in their own "sphere," because it embraced more of the everyday world. At the same time, values now known as "female," such as morality, virtue, and honesty, were increasingly being held up to all American people as standards to which they should aspire. The growing acceptance of women as moral guardians, which the works of the domestic novelists fostered, resulted in a feminization of American cultural values. This in turn gave women a measure of potency and prestige. Women quickly learned to wield their new position in order to protest and to enlarge the idealized model of what women should be.

Education was a primary focus for many women who desired enhanced status and increased opportunities. Catharine Beecher was especially active in attempting to reform women's education. Throughout the 1820s, Beecher ran the Hartford Female Seminary with her sister, Mary. During these years, she proposed that schools for women be endowed, argued that teachers' assignments be limited to a few fields, and advocated the training of young women in domestic science and teaching. In the 1830s, Beecher established the Western Female Institute in Cincinnati, where she collaborated with William H. McGuffey on his famous "readers," joined the temperance movement, and wrote extensively about women's domestic sphere, although she herself had decided not to marry. Beginning in the 1840s, Beecher supported herself by public lecturing and writing on the cause of women's education. She crusaded for teachers to be sent to the West and for normal schools to be established in frontier regions. She was responsible for organizing missionary societies to send female teachers westward and founded a number of women's schools, such as the Dubuque Female Seminary in Iowa, throughout the West.

Through her active and vigorous career, Beecher never strayed from her conviction that women were by nature domestic creatures. Her schools trained women as teachers before marriage and as homemakers after. Her curriculum stressed health, home economics, English, and arithmetic. Beecher avoided "higher" subjects such as mathematics and philosophy because she believed that they would weaken the female constitution and interfere with a woman's desire and ability to bear children. In her many books, such as the extremely popular *A Treatise on Domestic Economy* that appeared in 1841, Beecher offered household hints and recipes, and encouraged women to abandon stays, corsets, and other unhealthy, but fashionable, practices. Neither a feminist nor a suffragist, Beecher devoted her career to elevating the prestige and proficiency of women as teachers and homemakers.

Mary Lyon of Massachusetts held a slightly different view of women's education. Dissatisfied with her own meager training, Lyon decided in 1834 to found the first women's college in the United States. She wrote: "My heart has so yearned over the adult female youth in the common walks of life, that it has sometimes seemed as if there was a fire shut up in my bones." Indeed, she pursued with a fiery zeal her plan for "a residential seminary to be founded and sustained by the Christian public." She personally appealed to women for "five or ten dollars of hard-earned money, collected by the slow gains of patient industry." Although as an unmarried woman she was criticized for traveling alone, she persevered, and in 1837, her college, Mount Holyoke, enrolled its first student. The three-year course of study included Latin, science, and anatomy at a cost of sixty dollars a year for tuition, room, and board. When Mary Lyon died in 1849, Mount Holyoke had attained a reputation as an outstanding teacher-training institution.

Almira Lincoln Phelps was another educator who urged women to widen the female sphere. In 1841, Phelps and her attorney husband took charge of the Patapsco Female Institute in Baltimore. Here she provided a role model of a woman of attainment for her students. She wrote several standard botany textbooks and many literary pieces. She became the second woman to be admitted to the American Association for the Advancement of Science. After her husband's death in 1849, Phelps ran the school by herself until her retirement at sixty-three. Her mission throughout her career was to help young women find their way to an independent identity and to help them prepare for achievement. She taught them that marriage was not crucial to a productive life and that there were many ways of eluding the limitations of "women's sphere" without admitting it.

Although all of these educational experiments were aimed at middle- and upperclass women, a few did concern themselves with indigent and delinquent women. The Lancaster (Pennsylvania) Industrial School for Girls offered moral instruction and vocational training for girls between the ages of seven and sixteen. The school also provided medical care, a temporary home, and an employment service. Unlike most other women's schools, Lancaster's purpose was to save the daughters of the poor from vice, rather than to urge fundamental changes in women's roles.

Along with revised thinking about women's education came innovative ideas concerning women's health. Catharine Beecher was one of the first to perceive that women's roles as wives and mothers demanded a robust physical condition, stamina, and endurance. She designed an appropriate exercise program for female students in her schools and regarded herself as the inventor of calisthenics during the 1840s. But Emma Willard, Sarah Josepha Hale, Mary Lyon, and Almira Phelps also sought to combat the American woman's poor state of health through exercise. They regularly prescribed activities to improve posture, gracefulness, and general health.

All of these educators, however, operated on the principle that women's bodies could sustain only a limited amount of moderate exercise. They were progressive in that they introduced the idea of exercise for women, but they were restrictive in that they promoted a firm belief in female weakness that bedeviled women's sports programs both then and now. Women were, for example, encouraged to ride horses, but only in "proper" riding dress and sidesaddle. *Godey's Lady's Book* stressed this idea, urging women always to preserve their feminine grace and delicacy while riding. Racing and riding to the hounds was definitely frowned upon, but, by the 1850s, women were allowed to compete in "female equestrian" events at county fairs.

Other acceptable sports for women during the 1840s and 1850s were pedestrianism or foot racing. In 1852, one American woman, Kate Irvine, even competed in a British race in which she covered 500 miles. Most ladies' journals recommended moderate walking and sedate dancing as acceptable exercises. They warned, however, that women proceed with caution, for when the body is "too much exercised, it is apt to produce ganglions on the ankle joints of delicate girls, as wind galls are produced on the legs of young horses who are too soon or too much worked."

Evidently, modifications in women's education were limited by prevailing beliefs. Even when women won the right to become teachers, they soon found that little liberation occurred. By 1860, one quarter of American teachers were women, while in Massachusetts nearly four fifths of teachers were female. Despite their numbers and importance, women teachers still worked under the direction of men, earned low wages, and had little opportunity for alternative employment. Women who sought an education were usually confronted with an unimaginative traditional curriculum. Unfortunately, although some changes were gradually taking place in women's education, most people still agreed with French commentator Jean-Jacques Rosseau: "The whole education of women ought to be relative to men. To please them, to be useful to them, to make themselves loved and honored by them, to educate them when young, to care for them when grown, to counsel them, to console them, and to make life sweet and agreeable to them—these are the duties of women at all times, and what should be taught them from their infancy."

Women's growing resistance to this notion of their roles was demonstrated not only by their attempts to reshape educational philosophy but also by their entry into the temperance movement. Taking their moral responsibilities very seriously, thousands of women joined the American Temperance Society's crusade during the 1820s. They either became members of men's temperance societies, where they soon found their participation strictly circumscribed, or they formed women's societies, in which they could vote, hold office, and set policy. These women's groups occasionally accepted black women as members, but frequently black women worked for the temperance cause within black associations. During these early years, women were engaged primarily in moral suasion to bring about temperance among drinkers.

Gradually, temperance women began to learn of the oppression and abuse that many wives and daughters suffered at the hands of drunken husbands. In addition, they began to recognize that women and children were economically dependent on men, and that alcoholic husbands could destroy their families. Thus, women began to see the problem of alcoholism as male and the solution as female. Yet they felt thwarted because, although they could indeed exercise their moral powers, they could not influence the political realm. As a result, when the temperance movement turned from moral suasion to legal prohibition of alcohol in the 1840s, women felt totally left out of the very cause that they now saw as their own.

Women temperance advocates initially responded to the change in policy by resisting the abandonment of moral suasion as a technique. But in 1846, when Maine passed the first statewide law to ban the manufacture and sale of alcoholic beverages, women were forced to accept legal prohibition as their goal. But how were they to bring about legal prohibition if they could not vote or hold office? This dilemma was resolved by women's decision to resort to increased female pressure that often included confrontation and extralegal force. Women joined the Daughters of Temperance in unprecedented numbers; by 1848, it was one of the largest organizations for women, with a membership of 30,000. They held women's temperance meetings, and major gatherings such as the Women's Temperance Convention that met in New York in 1852. They petitioned legislatures for prohibition legislation. They formed bands that prayed and sang hymns outside, or sometimes inside, saloons. And between 1852 and 1859, groups of women entered saloons and physically destroyed the liquor stock. In essence, respectable and influential women became vigilantes who brandished weapons ranging from petitions to hatchets. Their actions, including the violent assaults on saloons, were supported by their communities and groups of temperance men who saw women as protecting their homes and children in the only ways open to them.

Women's widespread participation in the temperance movement affected women more than it did the consumption of alcohol. Many of them became ardent feminists in response to their absolute lack of political power. A temperance journal, *The Lily*, edited by Amelia Bloomer, began as a newspaper dedicated to "temperance and literature," but by 1852, its new masthead stated that it was "devoted to the interests of women." Women who began their careers as reformers in the temperance crusade frequently ended them in the women's rights movement. Many of them also experienced an increasing enmity toward men, whom they saw as oppressors blocking them from their political rights, and often as morally weak alcoholics as well. At the same time, these women began to see themselves not as submissive domestic beings, but as aggressive, effective reformers. In general, the temperance movement caused large numbers of women to question their place and to challenge domestic ideology.

Women also sought identity and resisted domesticity through religious and moral reform activities. These groups accepted the domestic nature of women, yet counseled women to become assertive participants in shaping the cultural values of their communities. In other words, they offered women the opportunity to deviate from their roles without appearing to do so and to exercise a degree of influence, especially over amoral, or perhaps immoral, men.

For instance, evangelical religions granted women a measure of importance through religious conversions and membership in women's auxiliaries to missionary, tract, and Bible societies. They also offered women an increased voice in church affairs and no longer expected them to be the obedient followers of authoritarian ministers. Moreover, the hope of human perfectability was now held out to women in place of a former emphasis on their inherent evil as daughters of Eve. Several religious sects, notably Shakerism, Spiritualism, Christian Science, and Theosophy, particularly attracted women members because they additionally deemphasized the masculine nature of God, denied the need for a traditional male clergy, and argued that marriage and motherhood were not the only acceptable female roles.

Other similar groups emphasized the positive influence of women and the necessity for women to implement it. Female reform societies urged their members to exert active control over the sexual mores of their friends and neighbors. In 1834, a group of women reformers founded the New York Female Reform Society dedicated to the credo that "it is the imperious duty of ladies everywhere and of every religious denomination, to co-operate in the great work of moral reform." The society published a journal called *The Advocate* to denounce "sin" in all forms. It hired several ministers to aid the needy in hospitals, jails, almshouses, and brothels. And members personally stood vigils and prayed outside of brothels.

During the 1830s, such female reform societies proliferated rapidly and encompassed large numbers of women. In 1835, the Boston Female Moral Reform Society was founded by seventy women who soon brought in hundreds more women through rural auxiliaries. By 1837, the New York society counted 250 auxiliaries and 15,000 members. Other local societies in New York often included several hundred members each. In 1840, when the New York group organized into the national American Female Moral Reform Society, its auxiliaries numbered 555.

Female reform societies used many innovative techniques, especially "visiting." Women reformers sang hymns and prayed at brothels, almshouses, and jails. They talked with prostitutes, the ill, and the poverty-stricken. And they solicited data and cases relating to sexual abuse and other ills. In addition to visiting, moral reformers petitioned state legislatures and lobbied for reform legislation. They also opened homes as refuges for women in need. In New York, this took the form of a House of Reception, a home for prostitutes. In Boston, a Home for Unprotected Girls, a Refuge for Migrant Women, and an Asylum for the Repentant were opened.

Other women attempted to improve American society by participating in Utopian experiments dedicated to alternate forms of labor and products. Brook Farm, outside of Boston, drew the support of the Transcendentalist, Margaret Fuller. Scottish-born reformer, Frances Wright, founded her own agricultural commune, Nashoba, in Tennessee. Other societies experimented with alternate forms of marriage. Oneida, founded in upstate New York in 1847, practiced complex marriage in which all members cohabited with each other and cared for the children as a group. On the other hand, the Shakers, founded by Mother Ann Lee, tried to free women from the handicaps of marriage and childcare by practicing celibacy. Women's voluntary associations were also becoming very active in America, especially in urban areas that faced such growing evils as poverty, crime, and prostitution. Female benevolence accounted not just for simple charity efforts, but also for the creation of complex, influential institutions and organizations. Sarah Josepha Hale's Boston Seaman's Aid Society was an example. Originally designed to help the bereft widows of seamen support themselves, it grew into a non-profit business, vocational training program, school, and home. Similarly, the Providence (Rhode Island) Employment Society began in the 1830s by trying to help exploited seamstresses and soon turned into a small garment business that paid fair wages and provided good working conditions. Such voluntary associations were usually formed as corporations with boards of directors, treasurers and other officers, and public relations programs.

Women's voluntary organizations not only dispensed charity, but drew women out of their homes, trained them in a large variety of business positions, and helped to turn women's morality into a paid vocation. Susan B. Anthony and other critics lamented the dirty work of society being left to women. "Men like to see women pick up the drunk and falling. . . . That patching business is 'woman's proper sphere,'" Anthony complained. But other women recognized the transforming power of voluntary associations on women. In 1841, writer and abolitionist Lydia Maria Child argued that such organizations "have changed the household utensil into a living energetic being." In another situation, the Utopian community of Oberlin, Ohio, encouraged women to enhance their powers through advanced education. This philosophy led in 1833 to the first coeducational college in the nation, Oberlin College.

Not all women who resisted the prevailing model of womanhood did so through such generally acceptable areas as literature, education, temperance reform, and religion. Some were willing to attack male bastions such as medical practice directly. They were disgusted with the philosophy of male midwives illustrated by the professor of midwifery who, in 1848, stated: "I hope the day is far distant when the spectacle shall be seen in our hospitals of troops of women waiting in succession for a public examination of their genitalia, in the presence of large classes of medical practitioners and students of medicine. I regard this public sentiment as to the sanctity of the female modesty and chastity as one of the strong safeguards of our spontaneous public probity—for woman, and man's respect and love for her, are truly at the basis, and are the very cornerstone, of civilization and order." He later responded in outrage to an explicit newspaper advertisement: "Who wants to know or ought to know that the ladies have abdomens and wombs but us doctors. When I was young, a woman had no legs even, but only feet, and possibly ankles: now forsooth, they have utero-abdominal supporters, not in fact only, but in the very newspapers!"

For thousands of women who relied on patent medicines heavy with opium, morphine, or alcohol, rather than seek treatment from unenlightened male physicians, modification of the medical establishment seemed absolutely necessary. In 1835, Harriot K. Hunt began practicing as a "female physician" in Boston after having completed an apprenticeship. Hunt was derided and, in her words, "entirely shut out from the medical world." Despite the obstacles, she practiced for over four decades, always educating herself as medical colleges were closed to women.

Elizabeth Blackwell was the first woman to successfully challenge this exclusion policy. In 1847, she applied to many medical schools, but was rejected by every one. Finally, the students of Geneva College in New York voted to accept her application as a joke. Unaware of the spoof, Blackwell entered Geneva in November, 1847, and began a long, lonely course of study. She was ostracized by the local people as queer and immoral and was barred from classroom demonstrations that involved human anatomy.

Upon receiving her medical degree in 1849, Blackwell sailed for England to seek further training. After many rejections, she finally found a less-than-suitable place as a student midwife in Paris. Here she lost the sight of one eye from disease, thus ending any possibility of a career as a surgeon. In 1850, she was admitted to St. Bartholomew's Hospital in London, where she was allowed to practice all branches of medicine except gynecology and pediatrics.

In 1851, Blackwell returned to New York. Shortly after her arrival, she wrote to her sister Emily that "a blank wall of social and professional antagonism faces a woman physician and forms a situation of singular and painful loneliness, leaving her without support, respect, or professional counsel." Despite discrimination, Blackwell opened a private dispensary that, in 1857, was incorporated as the New York Infirmary and College for Women. This hospital was conducted largely by women. Blackwell's sister Emily and Maria Zakrzewska, both of whom had earned medical degrees with her encouragement, helped Blackwell. Together, they treated patients, trained nurses, and repelled outraged townsfolk who occasionally even threw rocks through the windows.

After 1859, Blackwell lectured in England on medicine as a profession for women. Her name was placed on the British Medical Register, and she was welcomed in the very hospitals that had earlier refused to admit her. She finally settled in England, her place of birth, where she founded the National Health Society in 1871 and began to lecture on gynecology in 1875. She was not only the first woman doctor in the United States, but was one of the first physicians to work in public health and to stress preventative medicine.

As more women moved into medical practice during the mid-nineteenth century, they tended to see their constituencies as women and children. They also differed from male doctors in their emphasis on holistic treatments. Although women doctors were not necessarily feminists, they were often more sympathetic to women's growing demand for birth control information than were male doctors.

Changes in the American economy and an emphasis on Republican Motherhood made large families increasingly undesirable. A decline in the birth rate from an average of 7 in 1800 to 5.4 in 1850 demonstrated women's willingness to use birth control methods, such as coitus interruptus and an improved rubber condom, a result of the development of vulcanization of rubber in 1843. A few outspoken women, such as reformer Frances Wright, publicly advocated the practice of birth control. By the 1840s, there was a dramatic rise in the abortion rate, especially among married women. These trends culminated in the first explicit demand for birth control information by the women's rights movement in the 1840s. They issued a call for "Voluntary Motherhood," arguing that women who chose to bear children would be better mothers than those who were denied the choice.

The early birth control movement manifested a growing desire of many women to exercise control over their bodies and lives. It was becoming evident that numerous women did not wish to be confined to a life exclusively dedicated to wife- and motherhood, nor were they willing to accept their dependency on men. As a result, many different types of women began to speak out on their own behalf.

During the reform era between 1837 and 1861, a number of working women began to question the dominant ideology of domesticity and True Womanhood. One of these, Harriet Farley, a former mill operative at Lowell, even became an avowed women's rights advocate. In 1850, Farley wrote: "It has been impossible for me to consider so long the 'Rights and Duties of Mill-Girls' without opening my eyes to the vista just beyond the rights and duties of woman." She deplored the socialization of "masculine" men and "feminine" women that ignored the common ground between the two genders. She argued that agitation and education were necessary to achieve revision of these practices, and strongly supported the actions of women's rights conventions in creating public awareness of the issues involved. Farley maintained that "every thing that is really strengthening, elevating, enlarging, a woman wants—a woman needs." In her view, women could support themselves without losing their womanhood. "I have seen that they do not become less worthy and interesting when they become more useful and independent," she observed.

Unlike Farley, the majority of employed women during this period dealt with their frustrations and problems in less philosophical and more immediate ways. Their campaigns for working women's rights focused on higher wages, shorter hours, and improved working conditions. The Panic of 1837 caused a depression that lasted five years. Wages fell and unemployment spread. Bread riots were common in New York and other major cities. By 1845, most women were back to work but still earned less than two dollars per week. By 1850, there were 181,000 women employed in manufacturing and untold thousands more working as pieceworkers, domestic servants, and prostitutes. Unemployed women workers were forced to seek assistance from benevolent women's societies and other charity organizations. In New York City, one of the earliest of these was the "Mother Society," devoted to helping poor blacks and unemployed black women.

Most working women during the 1840s and 1850s were convinced that some type of organization was needed to correct the many problems that they faced. But society in general, and male union members in particular, frowned upon their participation in unions. Unwilling to accept the reality of women's employment, these people hoped that women workers would soon return to their "proper" places in the home. Working men also tended to fear women because they accepted low wages. These men did not yet realize that organizations of both women and men might establish fair wages for all workers.

Prejudice did not prevent women workers from joining men's unions, forming their own organizations, and participating in strikes. In 1845, the shoebinders at Lynn established a Producers Cooperative. In 1860, 500 men and 1,000 women held a huge rally during a strike. In the middle of a terrible blizzard, the meeting attracted 1,800 women who cheered the reading of a special poem, "The Song of the Shoemakers Strike." Some 20,000 more workers throughout New England joined this labor protest, known as "The Revolution in the North." It is unclear whether the strike brought about any actual gains, but it did provide the shoebinders with the organizational experience to found the Daughters of St. Crispin some years later.

During the late 1840s and 1850s, women workers in the clothing, shoe, wool, straw hat, printing, and other industries repeated these early attempts at organization and walkouts many times. Household workers and home pieceworkers had little opportunity to organize, strike, or otherwise to protect themselves from exploitation. Many made ends meet by taking aid from charitable societies and hiring out their children. Others turned to prostitution. In 1858, it was estimated that there were 6,000 prostitutes in New York City, one for every 64 adult males. Over half of these women had earned one to two dollars a week as seamstresses, dressmakers, hat trimmers, milliners, tailoresses, servants, and factory workers before becoming prostitutes. Sixty-three percent of them were born in other countries.

This latter statistic points at the tremendous problems immigrant women had in finding employment. Usually lacking industrial skills, forced to work at less than subsistence wages, and often unable to speak English, these women were exploited unmercifully by employers. Many of them became pieceworkers or domestic servants at unbelievably low wages. During the 1840s, one quarter of a million women, or one tenth of the adult female population, worked as domestics. The majority of these workers were Irish immigrants. Many other Irish women worked in the needle trades or as prostitutes. Stranded in urban areas by their lack of funds, Irish and large numbers of other immigrant women were unable to migrate to rural areas where they might put their agricultural skills to use. Chinese women were in a more difficult situation. Imported after 1840 primarily as prostitutes, Chinese women were a profitable commodity. Families often sold their daughters into servitude or were duped into parting with them. Other Chinese families survived only because of the meager wages earned in America. This sordid practice was encouraged by employers who did not want to pay Chinese laborers adequate wages to support a family or encourage permanent Chinese settlement. By the 1850s, Chinese societies known as *tongs* regularly supplied West Coast brothels with Chinese women. Chinese prostitution created miserable lives for the women involved, exacerbated anti-Chinese sentiment, and contributed to the devaluation of women and their labor.

Problems of laboring women were not quite as pressing in farm work. Those women, both immigrant and native born, who did migrate to western agricultural regions from the 1830s onward were quick to seize the limited opportunities that they found. Despite landholding policies that favored men, women could own land and participate in agriculture. Often these were widows, women with disabled husbands, and single women. By the early 1860s, one observer noted:

> We have heard of women in Western New York, Ohio and Michigan, that not only carry on farms but do the outdoor work, as tilling, reaping, etc. There are two sisters in Ohio who manage a farm of 300 acres: and two other sisters, near Media, Pennsylvania that conduct as large a farm. Mrs. D. owns a farm, and does not disdain to graft fruit trees, superintend their planting, gather fruit, send it to market, etc.: and she realizes a handsome profit.

Young women worked on farms as hired laborers during the three decades preceding the Civil War. These hired girls were often newly arrived immigrant women who did not disdain field work. The number of women working as "hired hands" increased as specialization developed. Wheat, corn, and dairy farms all demanded hired labor, both female and male. In 1857, the *Illinois Farmer* stated: "We want a supply of young women from the butter regions of Eastern States to come here and also from the Dairy Districts of England, Scotland, Ireland, and Germany." Black, immigrant, and poor women in particular were recruited for field work, but it was considered appropriate work for all women during periods of labor shortages.

In the South during these years, women were even more active in agricultural work. Historian Keith L. Bryant, Jr. maintains that white women on small tobacco, cotton, and subsistence farms regularly joined men in planting crops, weeding, and harvesting. Women of the middle-class yeomanry played a significant economic role in the family and frequently participated in making economic decisions. In addition, they transformed the raw materials of the fields into finished goods and provided cash income through the sale of their surplus products. Southern women gained property rights in several states during the 1850s, and common practice often protected their ownership of land, looms, cattle, and furniture. Yeoman women usually chose their own mates and often determined the number of children that they would bear. Some abandoned abusive, negligent, or lazy husbands, while many others served as teachers and exhorters. These middle-class southern women were important economic and moral forces whose assertiveness precluded patriarchy in their families.

Of course, the black slave women who provided similar labor on the larger farms and plantations were not in such enviable positions. Their situations did demand immediate attention from reformers. As property themselves, slave women could not own anything. They usually had no right to choose their mates or the number of children they bore. They had no control over their bodies being used for sexual or breeding purposes. They could not desert abusive husbands but might be torn from loving husbands through sale. The threat of physical punishment forced them immediately to accept a new spouse after the sale or death of a mate in order to keep producing children.

One of the few considerations slave women received was an occasional lightened work load while pregnant. One Virginia planter warned his overseers that "breeding wenches you must be Kind and Indulgent to, and not force them when with child upon any service or hardship that will be injurious to them." When not pregnant, however, slave women were expected to maintain an exhausting work schedule. They worked at jobs and performed all the usual domestic chores for their own families. In the fields, slave women sowed, hoed, and picked cotton, hoed and milled corn, and worked in lumbering, construction, and roadbuilding. They were expected to take part in all necessary tasks from plowing to building fences.

In 1853, an observer in South Carolina saw male and female slaves carrying manure containers on their heads to fields where they applied it by hand to the earth around cotton plants. In North Carolina, he observed women hoeing, shoveling, and cutting down trees to create roadbeds. Slave women were also sometimes hired out to cotton and woolen mills, sugar refineries, and tobacco factories. In 1860, about 5,000 slave women were so employed. Only about 5 percent of black slave women attained the relatively privileged status of house servant, serving as household slaves, nursemaids, and wet nurses. Aged slave women also worked hard at such tasks as sewing, weaving, spinning, canning, and caring for babies and young children whose mothers were in the fields. In addition, these aged "grannies" often served as nurses and midwives.

Slave women frequently rebelled against their heavy work loads. "She'd git stubborn like a mule and quit." Or she "chopped" the overseer across his head with her hoe or ran away into the woods to hide as a "truant." One Florida woman even chopped her overseer to death after a reprimand. Some women became concubines and mistresses to escape heavy labor. Others would "sham," that is, claim aches and disabilities due to their menstrual cycle or pregnancy. Another more subtle rebellion was the slave woman's adherence to the traditional division of labor within her home. By maintaining the customary roles and tasks of wife and mother, the slave woman could mock her owner's treatment of her as a man in the fields or foundry. Also, by acting as the force that held the family together in the face of daily adversity or that formed new kinship ties in times of crisis, a slave woman defied her owner's casual attitudes toward the institutions of marriage and family among slaves. By preserving her family from the dehumanizing aspects of slavery, black women were engaged in the ultimate revolt against the system.

By 1860, the population of the South included 7,033,973 whites, 258,000 free blacks, and 3,838,765 black slaves. Even though the constitutional ban on importing slaves went into effect in 1808, the slave system in the South had increased, primarily through smuggling and breeding. The latter method created an additional evil for black women, who were sold as "breeding wenches" and were expected to produce as many children as possible. Other slave women were sexually exploited by their masters. In Linda Brent's *Incidents in the Life of a Slave Girl*, edited by Lydia Maria Child in 1861, a tale of cruelty and licentiousness emerged. The author claimed that her master told her that "I was his property; that I must be subject to his will in all things." Such evils were further exacerbated by whites, whose fears of revolts grew as the numbers of slaves increased. They tightened the codes that restricted the behavior of their chattels and expanded the patrols that enforced such codes.

The dismal situation of slave women was described by Frances Kemble, a distinguished English actress who married a Georgia planter. Of her time spent on a plantation in 1838 and 1839, Kemble wrote: "It appears to me that the principal hardships fall to the lot of the women." Black slave women continually appealed to Kemble to lighten their work, soften their punishments, and extend their time of rest after childbirth to the customary four weeks. She felt overwhelmed by their stories, especially a particularly dismal one involving a woman who had borne sixteen children, fourteen of whom were dead, and had been lashed by "a man with a cowhide [who] stands and stripes" slaves. Kemble wrote: "I give you the woman's words. She did not speak of this as of anything strange, unusual, or especially horrid and abominable: and when I said: Did they do that to you when you were with child? she simply replied: Yes, missis." Outraged, Kemble added: "To all this I listen—I am Englishwoman, the wife of the man who owns these wretches, and I cannot say: That thing shall not be done again. I remained choking with indignation and grief long after thay had all left me to my most bitter thoughts."

Kemble's reactions to the slave system reflected the attitudes of many other plantation mistresses. Although some southern women did defend slavery as sanctioned by the Bible and protective of supposedly childlike blacks, Harriet Martineau claimed in the mid-1830s that she "never met with a lady of southern origin who did not speak of slavery as a sin and acurse the burden which oppressed their lives." Plantation wife Mary Boykin Chestnut also believed that most planters' wives were abolitionists at heart. And Maria J. McIntosh, daughter of an illustrious Georgia family, publicly aired her antislavery views in 1850 in a volume entitled *Woman in America*.

These white southern women had good reasons to hate slavery. They feared revolt, resented their husbands' sexual liaisons with black women, rebelled against their own heavy work loads in supervising and training black workers, and experienced guilt about oppressing black people. But the southern lady was hedged in by custom and economic dependence on her planter husband. She seldom dared to voice antislavery sentiments for fear of reprisal or abandonment. Moreover, as historian Catherine Clinton points out, southern women's social status and financial security depended on the continuation of the slave system, a factor that helped silence them on the issue. Circumscribed by the Cult of White Womanhood, the plantation woman confided her thoughts to her diary rather than to her spouse. In 1858, Georgian Ella Thomas recorded her conviction that "Southern Women are all at heart abolitionists" in her journal. She added: "I will stand to the opinion that the institution of slavery degrades the white man more than the Negro and exerts a most deleterious effect upon our children. . . . The happiness of homes is destroyed but what is to be done?"

While southern men engaged in "male" pursuits, such as business affairs, horse racing, cock fighting, gambling, drinking, and hunting, women kept their thoughts to themselves and worked alongside other women and with slaves. Contrary to the Magnolia Myth—the portrayal of leisured, hoopskirted southern belles—southern women devoted their time and energy to overseeing the house and its servants, conducting massive entertaining, providing medical care and schooling for all the people on the plantation, and supervising cooking, food processing, and the production of clothing.

These women did not support the pre–Civil War patriarchal system; they simply tolerated it when necessary. They strained against its dictates when possible. Some planter-class females employed the concept of Republican Motherhood to argue for improved educational opportunities. Their planter fathers and husbands concurred in the establishment of female academies because of their belief that educating their women would help to maintain the "tone" of the planter class. Women cherished their right to better educations, yet recognized that intellectual development would end with marriage, casting them into roles much like those that their mothers filled.

Besides modifying their views of women's education, antebellum Southerners also altered divorce laws. Women who sought divorce had to appear docile and submissive while substantiating their claim that they had been wronged by an adulterous, drunken, abusive, neglectful, or felonious husband. But once they proved their cases, these women were treated as capable beings and awarded substantial alimony payments, property, and control of their children. Women of means took advantage of the new laws and the more liberal attitudes they reflected. Between 1800 and 1860, twenty-one women in Alabama sued for divorce as opposed to seven men. Eleven of the wives were successful, while only two of the husbands obtained divorces. In Louisiana, sixteen wives sought divorces as compared to six husbands. Seven of the women were successful, while only one of the men was granted his request.

Evidently, many southern women of both the yeoman and planter classes challenged White Womanhood when and where they could during the 1840s and 1850s. Because they functioned in a conservative agrarian society, southern women were not as effective in breaking down barriers as were their northern counterparts, who had the advantage of operating in an industrial, relatively progressive world. Accordingly, not only the attack on women's sphere but the assault on the slave system had to come primarily from northern women.

One of the first northern women to assail the slave system was author Lydia Maria Child. Widely known for her editorship of *The Juvenile*

Miscellany, a children's magazine, and her authorship of *The Frugal Housewife,* a household hint book, Child published an early antislavery tract in 1833. Entitled *An Appeal for that Class of Americans Called Africans,* Child's book asked for justice and equality for black Americans. She pointed out that the "Negro woman is unprotected by either law or public opinion" and that she "must be entirely subservient to the will of their owner." After her readers turned against her for her unfeminine involvement in political matters, Child became the editor of the *National Anti-Slavery Standard* and devoted the rest of her career to the cause of abolitionism.

About the same time that Child's book appeared, a Quaker teacher, Prudence Crandall, accepted a black student into her Canterbury Female Boarding School in Connecticut. Local authorities warned Crandall that, if the young woman stayed, they would "ruin her school." She bravely replied, "Let it sink, then. I shall not turn her out." When all of Crandall's white students withdrew, she converted her school, with the help of abolitionist editor William Lloyd Garrison, into the High School for Young Colored Ladies and Misses, which opened in April 1833. A storm of protest erupted in the town of Canterbury. One group of irate citizens declared: "The Government of the United States, the nation with all its institutions, of right belong to the white men, who now possess them."

Crandall attempted to carry on with her school but was jailed during the summer of 1833 under a newly passed law that forbade the teaching of blacks in the state of Connecticut. Her case was aired around the world by the abolitionist press, and she was finally freed on a technicality. She returned to her school and to the continued harassment of townspeople who threw manure into her well, smashed the windows, threatened the students, and set fire to the building. After mob violence in September 1834, Crandall gave up. Recently married to an abolitionist minister, Crandall and her husband moved to Illinois. She maintained a lifelong interest in temperance reform and women's rights until her death in 1890.

Although these initial attempts to help blacks were abortive, they did alert many women to the need to form antislavery societies. Beginning in 1832, the formation of the New England Antislavery Society, the Connecticut Female Antislavery Society, and others in many states and regions marked the entry of women into the largely male abolitionist movement. Over one hundred societies had emerged by 1838. Because these women viewed slavery as a moral wrong, they felt compelled to exercise their moral powers against it. The Boston Female Antislavery Society declared: "As wives and mothers, as daughters and sisters, we are deeply responsible for the influence we have on the human race. . . . We are bound to urge men to cease to do evil and learn how to do good."

They also felt a growing sense of identification with black women. In

1837, abolitionist Angelina Grimké told a women's antislavery convention that black slave women were their "sisters" and "to us as women they have a right to look with sympathy for their sorrows, and effort and prayer for their rescue." They believed that if one woman was sexually degraded, then all women suffered and that if one mother was devalued, then all mothers lost stature. Women also felt a kind of kinship with slave women because of the restrictions on their lives as chattel. And abolitionist women hoped that, if they helped to free the slaves, liberation would be extended to white women as a logical and just outcome of their efforts.

At first, women's abolitionist societies were engaged in fund-raising and exhortation. They soon moved to more aggressive tactics, including organizing petition campaigns, holding national conventions, and speaking on the public platform. They increasingly resented the limitations placed on their activities due to their gender. In 1837, one woman's convention proclaimed: "The time has come for woman to move in that sphere which providence has assigned her, and no longer remain satisfied in the circumscribed limits which corrupt custom and a perverted application of Scripture have encircled her."

Women's increasing involvement in the abolitionist cause received national attention in the mid-1830s because of the activities of two southern-born women, Angelina and Sarah Grimké. Raised in Charlestown, South Carolina, as proper young ladies, both Grimkés grew up detesting slavery and resenting the restrictions inherent in White Womanhood. In 1821, at age twenty-eight, Sarah moved to Philadelphia and joined the Society of Friends. Angelina followed Sarah to Philadelphia and into the Quaker fold in 1829. Angelina soon joined the Philadelphia Female Anti-Slavery Society, noting in her diary, "I am confident not many years will roll by before the horrible traffic in human beings will be destroyed."

In 1836, Angelina's *Appeal to the Christian Women of the South* was published by the American Anti-Slavery Society. Copies of the pamphlet were publicly burned in the South, and the author was warned not to return to her home there. In that same year, Sarah also wrote a tract entitled *Epistle to the Clergy of the Southern States*. Both women began to lecture against slavery. Their willingness to lecture to mixed audiences of both women and men caused a great deal of public indignation. Undaunted, Angelina wrote a second pamphlet in 1837, *An Appeal to the Women of the Nominally Free States*.

The Grimké's lecturing and political reform activities created a women's-rights controversy. In 1837, a group of Congregationalist ministers in Massachusetts issued a "Pastoral Letter" protesting the sisters' unfeminine conduct. The letter said in part: "We invite your attention to the dangers which at present seem to threaten the female character with widespread and permanent injury. The appropriate duties and influence of women are clearly stated in the New Testament. The power of woman is her dependence, flowing from the consciousness of that weakness which God has given her for her protection."

Abolitionist leaders feared that the antislavery crusade would be jeopardized by the controversy and begged the Grimkés to ignore it. But the sisters replied that they could "not push abolitionism forward until we take the stumbling block out of the road." In 1838, Sarah stated their position in her pamphlet, *Letters on the Equality of the Sexes, and the Condition of Woman.* She minced no words in presenting the case: "I ask no favors for my sex. I surrender not our claim to equality. All I ask of our brethren is that they take their feet from off our necks, and permit us to stand upright on the ground which God has designed us to occupy." Shortly thereafter, Angelina married abolitionist reformer Theodore Dwight Weld. The newlywed couple and Sarah settled in New Jersey, where they continued to work for the causes of antislavery and women's rights.

Thousands of women followed the Grimkés' courageous example and joined the abolitionist movement during the 1840s and 1850s. Because they could not vote, they chose instead to petition Congress to pass laws restricting slavery. Petition-gathering was hard work that required travel and met with both scorn and apathy . Yet these women persevered and collected hundreds of thousands of signatures that Congress could not ignore. In addition to petitioning, abolitionist women lectured, wrote pamphlets, and helped slaves to escape to freedom via a network known as the Underground Railroad.

The most famous "conductor" of the Underground Railroad was Harriet Tubman. Born a slave in Maryland, Tubman fled to Philadelphia in 1849. In 1850, she returned to guide her sister and her two children to freedom and, in 1851, helped a brother and his family to escape. In all, Tubman is believed to have made nineteen trips into slave territory and freed as many as 300 people. Known as the "Moses of Her People," Tubman had a price of $40,000 on her head.

Tubman was not the only black woman to work for the liberation of slaves. Because they were often barred from white women's groups that believed in abolitionism but not equality, black women took matters into their own hands. Maria Miller Steward, a Connecticut free black, began to lecture publicly on behalf of her people during the early 1830s—a time when Frances Wright was one of the few woman brave enough to mount the public lecture platform and black lecturers were virtually unknown. Sarah Parker Remond, a free black woman from Salem, Massachusetts, lectured on the American antislavery cause in many European countries during the late 1850s and 1860s. She also pursued her own education and, in 1868, earned a medical degree in Italy. Ellen Craft, a fugitive slave, carried tales of the American slave system to England during the 1850s and 1860s.

One of the most well-known black female abolitionists was Charlotte Forten of Philadelphia. A teacher and author, Forten was also a founder of the Philadelphia Female Anti-Slavery Society. She was particularly active and effective in educating former slaves on the Sea Islands immediately after the Emancipation Proclamation in 1863. Her name became Grimké in 1878 when she married Francis James Grimké, a natural slave son of a brother of the abolitionist reformers, Angelina and Sarah Grimké.

Harriet Grimké Purvis, one of Charlotte's daughters, was also an active abolitionist. She and her husband were abolitionist leaders who used their Philadelphia home as a station on the Underground Railroad. In 1838 and 1839, Harriet served as a delegate to the Anti-Slavery Conventions of American Women. She continued to actively work for the causes of black Americans and women's rights until 1875.

Harriet's sister, Sarah, contributed poems and essays to the antislavery newspaper, *The Liberator,* composed a widely-sung antislavery song, "The Grave of the Slave," and tirelessly organized antislavery sewing circles and charity fairs. In 1837, she wrote the Grimké sisters that prejudice against her had made her "embittered." She felt that blacks were "innocent victims of prejudice for you are all well aware that it originates from dislike to the color of the skin much as from the degradation of Slavery." She added that she was trying to develop a "spirit of forebearance" for those who were racially biased.

Teacher Sarah Mapps Douglass was another leading black abolitionist. As early as the 1820s, she opened a school for black children in Philadelphia. In 1832, when the Pennsylvania legislature considered a bill that would have required all blacks to carry passes, Douglass became a political activist. "One short year ago, how different were my feelings on the subject of slavery!" she exclaimed. But, when racism indirectly threatened her own freedom, she determined "to use every exertion" in her power "to elevate the character of my wronged and neglected race." As a result, she became deeply involved in the Philadelphia Female Anti-Slavery Society and taught at the Institute for Colored Youth, where she was instrumental in training many of Philadelphia's public school teachers. After the Civil War, Douglass served in a leadership position with the Pennsylvania branch of the Freedman's Aid Commission and continued her innovative teaching career.

Other black female abolitionists were Frances Ellen Watkins Harper, a well-known lecturer, author, and reformer; Mary Ann Shadd Cary, a teacher, journalist, and lawyer; Maria W. Stewart, a lecturer, writer, and teacher; and Sarah Parker Remond, a speaker and author. Despite racism and sexism, these and other black women fought for the improvement of black Americans during the 1830s, 1840s, and 1850s. Discriminated against by white women's abolitionist societies, black women formed their own organizations dedicated to the cause of black freedom or joined racially integrated groups as "colored" members. They soon realized that an aversion to slavery on the part of white women did not mean that they would extend equality to black women. Black women were not represented in the National Convention of Female Anti-Slavery Societies and other groups.

Sojourner Truth was probably the most famous black woman reformer and lecturer of this period. Born a slave in New York and originally named Isabella, she fled from her owner in 1827, a year before slaves were freed in that state. In 1829, she arrived in New York City with two of her children and obtained work as a domestic servant. She became a preacher and was especially active in the effort to turn the city's many prostitutes to religion. In 1843, she took the name Sojourner Truth and set out on foot to preach throughout New England. She became an enthusiastic supporter of the abolitionist movement in 1846. She toured the Midwest lecturing against slavery in spite of threats and physical attacks. In Indiana, she bared her breast to disprove the allegations that she was really a man in disguise. In 1850, after experiencing constant discrimination as a female reformer, she took up the cause of women's rights. In 1852, at a women's rights meeting in Akron, Ohio, she delivered her famous "Ain't I A Woman" speech in which she pointed out that chivalry and True Womanhood were not very meaningful concepts to most women, especially black, laboring, and poor women. After emancipation, Truth argued adamantly for rights for black women as well as for white because she was convinced that "if colored men get their rights and not colored women theirs ... the colored men will be masters and it will be just as bad as it was before."

Sojourner Truth was far from alone in her frustrations. Many antislavery women, as well as women who supported temperance, moral reform, and other causes, chafed at the limitations they encountered. They had no political influence because they could not own property, vote, or hold office. They were condemned for speaking in public and disdained for entering the halls of Congress with their petitions. How were they to function as effective reformers without some weapons or power? And how were they to wield their moral force? If they were the moral guardians of society, then they must be able to exercise their powers. Women's experience with powerlessness reinforced lessons that they had been learning for over half a century. Since the early 1800s, women's voluntary associations, especially in the newly emerging urban areas of America, had been trying to deal with such problems as alcoholism and prostitution. They had come to recognize the value of reforms that would increase the rights of women. Now, numerous abolitionists and other women reformers added the issue of women's rights to their reform platforms between 1837 and 1861. For some, gaining rights was a practical matter—they simply wanted to proceed with their reforms. For others, achieving their rights was an ethical issue that would allow them to carry out their moral responsibilities to the nation.

The problems posed by women reformers came to a head in 1840, when the national antislavery organization split into male-only and male-female factions over the "woman question." The integrated group sent female delegates to a world antislavery convention in London in 1841. Here, the women were seated behind a curtain and denied the right to vote. When they walked out in indignation, they were joined by a number of sympathetic men. As a result of this upsetting incident, Lucretia Mott and Elizabeth Cady Stanton agreed that a women's protest meeting was needed in America. But it was not until 19 July 1848 that the first women's rights meeting was held in Seneca Falls, New York.

The chairperson of the Seneca Falls meeting was James Mott, Lucretia's husband. Elizabeth's husband, Henry Stanton, had fled in embarrassment. The meeting attracted approximately 300 people, including about 40 men. After many speeches, the delegates paraphrased the Declaration of Independence in a plea for equality and expanded rights for women, including the right to vote. It read: "We hold these truths to be self-evident: that all men and women are created equal: that they are endowed by their Creator with certain inalienable rights: that among these are life, liberty and the pursuit of happiness. The history of mankind is a history of repeated injuries and usurpations on the part of man toward woman, having in direct object the establishment of an absolute tyranny over her."

Although the demands issued at Seneca Falls in 1848 were met with unsparing ridicule in the press, many other similar conventions followed in both eastern and western states. In 1850, James Gordon Bennett of the New York Herald asked: "What do the leaders of the women's right conventions want? They want to be members of Congress, and in the heat of debate subject themselves to coarse jests and indecent language." Many people were sincerely puzzled by advocates of women's rights, especially when Amelia Bloomer, a temperance reformer, women's rights editor, and suffragist in Seneca Falls, began to wear a reform dress composed of a short skirt and Turkish-style pantaloons during the winter of 1850–1851. Bloomer and the other women who adopted the costume were expressing their desire for better health, freedom of movement, and even equality by freeing themselves from the dictates of fashion. But, due to the controversy that the Bloomer outfit created, most women had abandoned it by the end of the decade.

Women's rights may have appeared to be a foolish and trivial issue to some people, but for its female and male advocates it was serious and far-reaching in its implications. Seeing the ideal family as a partnership rather than a patriarchy, women's rights supporters campaigned for legal changes that would allow married women to own property. As early as 1829, the *American Monthly Magazine* argued that the present restrictive laws made husbands greedy and wives mean and concealing. In 1839, the state of Mississippi passed the first Married Women's Property Law.

Soon, many women's rights advocates began to promote modification of women's property laws, particularly a Jewish woman of Polish birth named Ernestine Rose. First a temperance and abolitionist reformer, Rose had become committed to women's rights by the 1840s. In New York, Rose circulated petitions and spoke for the newly introduced women's property bill. When it was finally passed in 1848, it was limited in scope but did mark the beginning of alterations in women's ownership of property. Shortly afterward, Pennsylvania passed a similar bill, largely because of the urgings of journalist and newspaper editor Jane Swisshelm.

Proponents of women's rights during the 1840s and 1850s were also eager to gain political privileges for women. They were outraged that the widely touted "democracy" that developed during the Age of Jackson applied only to white males and not to females. To these reformers, suffrage meant more than simply the right to cast a ballot. They saw women's entry into the public arena as the path to the larger goal of equality with men. They drew on the techniques learned through the abolitionist and other reform campaigns and appealed to activists in those areas for support.

The very women who seemed so intent on the extension of equality only occasionally encouraged black women to join in their crusade or discouraged their participation altogether. Although many black women seem to have considered antislavery a more pressing cause, some did become feminists. For example, abolitionist and journalist Mary Ann Shadd Cary was also a feminist. Although the involvement of black women in the women's rights and feminist movements has been generally overlooked, there is evidence that they were active participants.

In the process of defending their demands, women's rights leaders developed an intricate ideology during the 1840s and 1850s. It was derived from three sources. First, existing doctrines of the American Revolution contributed ideas of equality, human perfectibility, and the right of citizens to participate in their own governance. In 1848, the Seneca Falls delegates utilized the Declaration of Independence.

Second, the philosophies of British reformers fed into the American women's rights crusade. In 1792, Mary Wollstonecraft, an English author, published her *Vindication of the Rights of Women*. This book was one of the first arguments for the equality of women and was widely read in America. In the 1830s, Frances Wright's lectures offered valuable insights into the topics of equality, improved education, divorce, and birth control. And Frances Kemble's speeches recounting her life on a Georgia plantation, also published as a book entitled *Journal of a Residence on a Georgian Plantation* in 1863, supplied a firsthand account of the evils of the slave system and the oppression of slave and white southern women.

Third, American writers and speakers offered a variety of perspectives and philosophies. Margaret Fuller, known as the "high priestess" of the Transcendentalist movement, addressed the issue of equality. As editor of the Transcendentalist journal, *The Dial,* during the 1840s, Fuller maintained that women should be allowed to expand their strengths and interests, just as men did. In 1845, Fuller's *Woman in the Nineteenth Century* developed the case for equality further. She stated: "I would have Woman lay aside all thought, such as she habitually cherishes, of being taught and led by men. I would have her free from compromise, from complaisance, from helplessness, because I would have her good enough and strong enough to love one and all beings, from the fullness, not the poverty of being." Fuller concluded: "Now there is no woman, only an overgrown child."

Elizabeth Cady Stanton concentrated her efforts on gaining the ballot for women. As an organizer of the Seneca Falls meeting in 1848, a founder of the Woman's Loyal League in 1863, and a candidate for Congress in 1866, Stanton believed that liberation lay in political participation. She disdained the idea of woman's sphere: "The talk of sheltering woman from the fierce storms of life is the sheerest mockery, for they beat on her from every point of the compass, just as they do on man, and with more fatal results, for he has been trained to protect himself, to resist, to conquer." During the 1840s and 1850s, Stanton also campaigned on behalf of abolitionism, temperance, education, and property rights for women. But because she was blocked by her father and husband and was burdened by the care of her children, she often had to rely on others to carry her messages.

Susan B. Anthony became Stanton's closest collaborator. Henry Stanton reportedly told Elizabeth, "You stir up Susan and she stirs up the world." Anthony did indeed prove herself to be an effective orator and an efficient organizer for temperance, abolitionism, and women's rights during the 1840s and 1850s. A Quaker schoolteacher and manager of the family farm, Susan B. Anthony, never married, was free to travel and speak. After meeting Elizabeth Cady Stanton in 1850, Anthony came to her for ideas and often helped her with the children and household chores in order to free her for a few hours of thought. Like Stanton, Anthony emphasized the right to vote. "Suffrage involves every basic principle of republican government, all our social, civil, religious, educational, and political rights," she maintained. "It is therefore germane to discuss every invidious distinction of sex in the college, home, trades and professions, in literature, sacred and profane, in the canon as well as in the civil law."

Lucy Stone also contributed to the ideology of women's rights. After attending Oberlin College in the 1840s, Stone became an abolitionist speaker and survived a drenching with a hose and a blow from a hurled prayerbook, among other indignities. She soon came to deplore the idea of Civil Death and the limitations that it placed on women. When she married Henry Blackwell in 1855, Stone kept her family name and entered into a well-publicized marriage contract with Blackwell. Their agreement read: "While acknowledging our mutual affection by publicly assuming the relationship of husband and wife, yet in justice to ourselves and a great principle, we deem it a duty to declare that this act on our part implies no sanction of, nor promise of voluntary obedience to such of the present laws of marriage, as refuse to recognize the wife as an independent, rational being, while they confer upon the husband an injurious and unnatural superiority, investing him with legal powers which no honorable man would exercise, and which no man should possess." Coming from a reforming family and himself committed to women's rights, Blackwell seemed to take the ensuing public derision in stride.

Lucretia Mott also came to women's rights through abolitionism. As a Quaker, Mott possessed a strong sense of self-worth that she could not reconcile with the degrading treatment she received as a female reformer. And as an official minister in the Society of Friends, she had a deep religious belief in justice and equality for all people. During the 1850s, she turned her Philadelphia home into an Underground Railroad "station" and, in addition to caring for six children, traveled extensively to lecture on abolitionism and women's rights. She frequently employed Biblical evidence to argue that the inferior status of women was neither natural nor divinely ordained. In 1849, Mott decried women's long-term bondage. Woman "has been so long subject to the disabilities and restrictions, with which her progress has been embarrassed, that she has become enervated, her mind to some extent paralyzed; and like those still more degraded by personal bondage, she hugs her chains." Rather than promoting woman suffrage, Mott concentrated on a new view of women as responsible, self-sustaining individuals.

The energy and ideas of these women's rights leaders helped create a dynamic and visible movement by the 1850s. Hundreds of women's rights meetings were held each year, and the "woman question" was widely and hotly debated. But there were many problems. Women's rights appealed primarily to white middle- and upperclass women. Consequently, the participants were neither numerous nor representative of the female population as a whole. Issues important to working, immigrant, poor, black, and American Indian women were ignored in favor of other larger concerns, such as equality and suffrage. In addition, women's rights advocates lacked effective means to pursue their objectives. Limited to speaking, writing, and petitioning, they often had difficulty getting their points across. To complicate matters further, few Americans were ready to take the matter of women's rights seriously. Finally, other national events tended to overshadow women's rights. The burgeoning settlement of the West, the Mexican War, 1846–1848, the Gold Rush in 1849, unprecedented industrial expansion, King Cotton and slavery, the Fugitive Slave Law of 1850 and the Underground Railroad, reformism, and a literary flowering known as the American Renaissance drew attention away from women's issues between 1837 and 1861.

Still, the groundwork of an American feminist movement was in place. In some ways, it was very rudimentary. Attention was focused on specific issues of women's rights rather than on the development of a more comprehensive feminist platform and consciousness. And, in rather simplistic terms, women's righters frequently identified men as the enemy rather than examining the structure of their society. Yet issues had been pinpointed and discussed, the public had been exhorted to increase its awareness of the ills afflicting women, and the accepted model of womanhood had been seriously challenged. In addition, women had learned organizational and speaking skills, attracted a number of male supporters, and forced legislators to accept their petitions. Although domesticity was still preached as the highest standard for American women, the emergent women's rights crusade had encouraged resistance to its actual acceptance on many fronts.

In 1861, the tremendous crisis of the Civil War would shatter American society, destroying institutions, revising customs, and reshaping the national scene as it progressed. Its effects would be felt by all Americans, particularly blacks and women. That the war radically changed the situation of blacks is a well-known fact. But, even though the war's impact on women is neither as well documented nor as widely recognized, it was significant and fascinating.

SUGGESTIONS FOR FURTHER READING

Albert, Judith Strong. "Margaret Fuller's Row at the Greene Street School: Early Female Education in Providence, 1837–1839." *Rhode Island History* 42 (May 1983): 43–55.

Basch, Norma. "Invisible Women: The Legal Fiction of Marital Unity in Nineteenth-Century America." *Feminist Studies* 5 (Summer 1979): 346–366.

———. "Equity vs. Equality: Emerging Concepts of Women's Political Status in the Age of Jackson." *Journal of the Early Republic* 3 (Fall 1983): 297–318.

Bednarowski, Mary Farrell. "Outside the Mainstream: Women's Religion and Women Religious Leaders in Nineteenth-Century America." *Journal of the American Academy of Religion* 48 (June 1980): 207–231.

Berg, Barbara J. *The Remembered Gate: Origins of American Feminism.* New York: Oxford University Press, 1978.

Berkin, Carol Ruth, and Mary Beth Norton, eds. *Women of America: A History.* Boston: Houghton Mifflin Company, 1979, 177–202.

Belding, Robert E. "The Dubuque Female Seminary." *The Palimpsest* 63 (March/April 1982): 34–41.

Brenzel, Barbara. "Lancaster Industrial School for Girls: A Social Portrait of a Nineteenth-Century Reform School for Girls." *Feminist Studies* 3 (Fall 1975): 40–53.

Bryant, Jr., Keith L. "The Role and Status of the Female Yeomanry in the Antebellum South: The Literary View." *Southern Quarterly* 18 (Winter 1980): 73–88.

Burnham, Dorothy. "The Life of the Afro-American Woman in Slavery." *International Journal of Women's Studies* 1 (July/August 1978): 363–377.

Campbell, John. "Work, Pregnancy, and Infant Mortality Among Southern Slaves." *Journal of Interdisciplinary History* 14 (Spring 1984): 793–812.

Censer, Jane Turner. "'Smiling Through Her Tears': Ante-Bellum Southern Women and Divorce." *American Journal of Legal History* 25 (January 1981): 24–47.

Clinton, Catherine. "Equally Their Due: The Education of the Planter Daughter in the Early Republic." *Journal of the Early Republic* (Spring 1982): 39–60.

―――. *The Other Civil War: American Women in the Nineteenth Century.* New York: Hill and Wang, 1984. Chapters 2–4, 6–8.

Conrad, Susan P. *Perish the Thought: Intellectual Women in Romantic America, 1830–1860.* New York: Oxford University Press 1976.

Davis, Angela. "Reflections on the Black Woman's Role in the Community of Slaves." *The Black Scholar* 3 (December 1971): 3–15.

Douglas, Ann. *The Feminization of American Culture.* New York: Alfred A. Knopf, 1979.

DuBois, Ellen Carol. *Feminism and Suffrage: The Emergence of an Independent Women's Movement in America, 1848–1869.* Ithaca: Cornell University Press, 1978.

Eckhardt, Celia Morris. *Fanny Wright: Rebel in America.* Cambridge, MA: Harvard University Press, 1984.

Foner, Philip S., and Josephine F. Pacheco. *Three Who Dared: Prudence Crandall, Margaret Douglass, Myratilla Miner-Champions of Antebellum Black Education.* Westport, CT: Greenwood Press, 1984.

Friedman, Jean E., and William G. Shade, eds. *Our American Sisters: Women in American Life and Thought.* Lexington, MA: D. C. Heath and Company, 1982. Part II.

Ginzberg, Lori D. "Women in an Evangelical Community: Oberlin, 1835–1850." *Ohio History* 89 (Winter 1980): 78–88.

Greene, Dana. "'Quaker Feminism': The Case of Lucretia Mott." *Pennsylvania History* 48 (April 1981): 143–154.

Groneman, Carol. "Working-Class Immigrant Women in Mid-Nineteenth Century New York: The Irish Woman's Experience." *Journal of Urban History* (May 1978): 255–273.

Hardesty, Nancy A. *Women Called to Witness: Evangelical Feminism in the 19th Century.* Nashville: Abingdon Press, 1984.

Hersh, Blanche G. *The Slavery of Sex: Feminist-Abolitionists in Nineteenth Century America.* Urbana: University of Illinois Press, 1978.

Hirata, Lucie Cheng. "Free, Indentured, Enslaved: Chinese Prostitutes in Nineteenth-Century America." *Signs* 5 (Autumn 1979): 3–29.

Hoffman, Nancy. *Woman's "True" Profession: Voices from the History of Teaching.* Old Westbury, NY: Feminist Press, 1981.

Hudson, Winthrop S. "Early Nineteenth-Century Evangelical Religion and Women's Liberation." *Foundations* 23 (April/June 1980): 181–85.

James, Edward T., ed. *Notable American Women, 1607–1950: A Biographical Dictionary.* Cambridge, MA: Harvard University Press, 1971.

Jones, Jacqueline. "'My Mother Was Much of a Woman': Black Women, Work, and the Family under Slavery." *Feminist Studies,* 8 (Summer 1982): 235–269.

Kelley, Mary. "The Sentimentalists: Promise and Betrayal in the Home." *Signs* 4 (Spring 1979): 434–446.

———. *Private Woman, Public Stage: Literary Domesticity in Nineteenth-Century America.* New York: Oxford University Press, 1984.

Kerber, Linda K., and Jane DeHart Mathews, eds. *Women's America: Refocusing the Past.* New York: Oxford University Press, 1982. Part IIa.

Lauer, Jeanette C., and Robert H. Lauer. "The Language of Dress: A Sociohistorical Study of the Meaning of Clothing in America." *The Canadian Review of American Studies* 10 (Winter 1979): 305–323.

———. "The Battle of the Sexes: Fashion in 19th Century America." *Journal of Popular Culture* 8 (Spring 1980): 581–89.

Lerner, Gerda. *The Grimké Sisters from South Carolina: Pioneers for Woman's Rights and Abolition.* New York: Schocken Books, 1971.

———. ed. *Black Women in White America: A Documentary History.* New York: Random House, 1973.

———. "The Political Activities of Antislavery Women." 112–28 In *The Majority Finds Its Past,* edited by Gerda Lerner, 112–28. New York: Oxford University Press, 1979.

Morantz, Regina Markell, and Sue Zschoche. "Professionalism, Feminism, and Gender Roles: A Comparative Study of Nineteenth-Century Medical Therapeutics." *Journal of American History* 67 (December 1980): 568–588.

Nelson, Margaret K. "Vermont Schoolteachers in the Nineteenth Century." *Vermont History* 49 (Winter 1981): 5–30.

Rosenberg, Rosalind. *Beyond Separate Spheres: Intellectual Roots of Modern Feminism.* New Haven: Yale University Press, 1982.

Ryan, Mary P. "The Power of Women's Networks: A Case Study of Female Moral Reform in Antebellum America." *Feminist Studies* 5 (Spring 1979): 66–85.

———. *Womanhood in America from Colonial Times to the Present.* New York: New Viewpoints, 1979. Chapter 3.

Scott, Anne Firor. "Almira Lincoln Phelps: The Self-Made Woman in the Nine-teenth Century." *Maryland Historical Magazine* 75 (September 1980): 203–216.

Sklar, Kathryn Kish. *Catharine Beecher: A Study in American Domesticity.* New York: W. W. Norton and Company, 1973.

———. "The Founding of Mount Holyoke College." In *Women of America: A History,* edited by Carol Ruth Berkin and Mary Beth Norton, 177–202. Boston: Houghton Mifflin Company, 1979.

Terborg-Penn, Rosalyn. "Discrimination Against Afro-American Women in the Women's Movement, 1830–1920." In *The Afro-American Woman: Struggles and Images* edited by Sharon Harley and Rosalyn Terborg-Penn, 17–27. Port Washington, New York: Kennikat Press, 1978.

Tyrrell, Ian R. "Women and Temperance in Antebellum America, 1830–1860." *Civil War History* 28 (June 1982): 128–52.

Vertinsky, Patricia. "Sexual Equality and the Legacy of Catharine Beecher." *Journal of Sport History* 6 (Spring 1979): 38–49.

Walsh, Mary R. *"Doctor's Wanted: No Women Need Apply": Sexual Barriers in the Medical Profession, 1835–1975.* New Haven: Yale University Press, 1977.

Walters, Ronald C. "The Erotic South: Civilization and Sexuality in American Abolitionism." In *Procreation or Pleasure? Sexual Attitudes in Amerian History* edited by Thomas L. Altherr, 87–98. Malabar, FL: Robert E. Kreiger Publishing Company, 1983.

Weiner, Nella Fermi. "Of Feminism and Birth Control Propaganda, 1790–1840." *International Journal of Women's Studies* 3 (September/October 1980): 411–430.

White, Deborah Gray. "The Lives of Slave Women." *Southern Exposure* 12 (November/December 1984): 32–39.

———. *Ar'n't I a Woman? Female Slaves in the Plantation South.* New York: W. W. Norton & Co., Inc., 1984.

Woloch, Nancy. *Women and the American Experience.* New York: Alfred A. Knopf, 1984. Chapters 5–8.

After Harriet Tubman escaped from slavery in 1849, she became known as the "Moses of Her People" for her successful activities with the Underground Railroad. During the Civil War, Tubman was the only black person to serve with the Union armies as a scout and a spy. Courtesy of the Library of Congress, Washington, D.C.

CHAPTER 5

"Womanly Strength of the Nation": The Civil War and Reconstruction 1861–1877

I N April 1861, the American nation split into two warring factions, the United States of America and the Confederate States of America. Two major questions were at issue: the continuation and extension of the black slave system and the political unity of the northern and southern states. During four long years of hostilities lasting until 1865, the South lost some 265,000 lives and the North, 364,000. Industrialization made widespread and efficient slaughter possible for the first time. Rather than glorious or romantic, the Civil War was destructive and terrifying. Its impact changed the course of American history in many ways.

The Civil War and its aftermath not only shook American society and government to its foundations but had a marked influence on the lives and roles of American women. The model of womanhood, already somewhat unstable as a result of the many attacks by reformers, experienced further blows during the years of war and reconstruction. Yet the resiliency of the image was remarkable. Although it tottered a bit, it did not collapse and fall.

From the very beginning of the Civil War, women were drawn into the war effort by requests for huge amounts of foodstuffs, bandages, and other sanitary goods, which were being rapidly consumed primarily by ill-supplied military hospitals. During the spring of 1861, women began to congregate in homes, hotels, and churches to preserve fruits, roll bandages, sew shirts, and organize charity fairs and other fund-raising events to collect money with which to buy supplies.

These women's groups quickly began to organize into aid societies and sanitary commissions. As early as April 1861, 3,000 New Yorkers met in Cooper Union to form the New York Central Association of Relief. Similar types of organizations appeared in many states, in which women served as officers and on the boards of directors and finance committees.

By the end of 1861, there were approximately 20,000 women's aid societies in the United States and the Confederacy.

These women's groups sent tremendous quantities of supplies to the front. Organized in 1862, the Weldon, Pennsylvania, society contributed $17,000 in goods in one year. In one month in 1863, the Center Ridge, Alabama, group sent "422 shirts, 551 pairs of drawers, 80 pairs of socks, 3 pairs of gloves, 6 boxes and a bale of hospital stores, 128 pounds of tapioca and $18 for hospital use." During these years, other local societies began to establish "refreshment saloons" in the North and "wayside homes" in the South to aid passing military personnel. Two Philadelphia saloons had dispensed more than $80,000 in supplies and served more than 600,000 meals by the beginning of 1864.

Frequently, representatives from women's groups traveled to the front to aid the administration of supply distribution. They attempted to organize the efforts of different women's groups, preventing duplicated deliveries on the one hand and shortages on the other. They also routed supply wagons away from roads used by troops and munitions. Annie Turner Wittenmyer of Keokuk, Iowa, served in this way as forwarding agent for aid societies throughout the state and, in 1862, was appointed as a State Sanitary Agent. Appalled by the black coffee, greasy bacon, and hardtack served to patients in the military hospitals, Wittenmyer began to campaign for "diet kitchens" that would serve healthful rations. In 1864, her first kitchen was established, and by the end of the war these kitchens had become an accepted feature of military hospitals. Near the end of the war, she turned her attention to the problem of war orphans and in 1865 persuaded the federal government to give several new buildings and many hospital supplies to the newly organized Iowa Orphans Home Association in Davenport, Iowa.

Besides supplying the troops and hospitals, women also nursed the wounded and dying. Nurses were often trained in the field since few nursing schools existed at that time. By the end of 1861, Dr. Elizabeth Blackwell had established a training program for nurses and applied for the position of Superintendent of Women Nurses. Dorothea Dix was given the job instead, partly because of the hostility against Blackwell as a female doctor. Dix recruited only women who were at least thirty years of age and "plain in appearance," a policy that caused great bitterness among younger women who were eager to contribute their services to the war effort.

Mary Ann Bickerdyke was a particularly well-known war nurse. Called "Mother" Bickerdyke, this Quaker woman gained a reputation as a tireless worker and fearless administrator in the nineteen battlefield hospitals in which she served between 1861 and 1865. A coworker of Bickerdyke's claimed that she was not afraid of anybody, including the high-ranking generals. "But Lord, how she works!" she marveled.

Another Civil War nurse, Hannah Ropes of Massachusetts, kept a diary during her service in 1862–1863 in a Washington hospital that offers insight into the life of the female nurse. In August 1862 she wrote: "We have just cleaned and dressed over a hundred men from the Harrison's Landing—poor, worn fellows!" A month later, she described a young man who was shot through the lungs yet survived the night. "We considered him the greatest sufferer in the house, as every breath was a pang," she commented. As a strong abolitionist, she explained that she could endure the hardships associated with nursing because "this is God's war. . . . The cause is that of the human race, and must prevail."

Mary Livermore, another Massachusetts war nurse, fought long and hard against the terrible conditions that she found in the military hospitals. After a tour of military hospitals in 1863, she instituted a letter-writing and canvassing campaign in Illinois to raise needed supplies. Her description of one of the hospitals in which she served graphically presents the difficult conditions: "It was a miserable place. . . . The cots were placed inside the tents, on unplanked ground. . . . The hospital swarmed with large green flies, and their buzzing was like that of a beehive. . . . Many of the patients did not lift their hands to brush away the flies that swarmed into eyes, ears, noses, and mouths."

The writings of Phoebe Yates Pember, a hospital matron near Richmond, indicated that conditions were no better in the Confederate hospitals. Railing especially against drunken surgeons, Pember also recorded incompetency, laziness, and discrimination against her as a woman administrator. By 1863, wartime prices were so high in Richmond and her salary so meager that, at night, she wrote for magazines or did copy work for the War Department to supplement it.

As a result of such dreadful conditions, yet another Civil War nurse, Clara Barton, eventually began to crusade for the establishment of the American Red Cross in the 1870s. Her wartime experiences convinced her of the need for a national, ongoing relief organization that would be able to offer aid during wars and other national disasters. The Civil War had taught her about corruption, lack of supplies, and carnage so great that, in her words, "I wrung the blood from the bottom of my clothing before I could step."

For their Herculean efforts, army nurses received compliments from many people ranging from wounded soldiers to President Lincoln himself. In 1892, the United States Congress finally granted them formal recognition of their inestimable services by giving them a pension of twelve dollars a month.

Women's contributions to medical hospitals also resulted in the establishment of several institutions dedicated to the training of women doctors. Neither the Union nor the Confederacy commissioned women physicians at the outbreak of the war. In 1861, Mary Walker applied to the

Union government as a medical doctor but was denied a commission until 1864. Although such women as Elizabeth and Emily Blackwell and Maria Zakrzewska practiced in the North and others such as Louisa Shepard and Elizabeth Cohen practiced in the South, there was widespread resistance to women doctors. During the war, however, many people began to recognize the medical competency of these doctors and to support the idea that women should have access to medical training. Such arguments for the active role of women in medical practice led to the founding of the Chicago Hospital for Women and Children and the New York Medical College for Women, both in 1863.

Women offered their talents on many other fronts as well. Some went to the fighting front as soldiers. Disguised as men, about 400 women fought in the Civil War between 1861 and 1865. Sarah Emma Edmonds of Michigan claimed that she served as a male nurse, spy, mail carrier, and soldier for two years, while Amy Clarke of Mississippi enlisted with her husband and continued to fight after he was killed at Shiloh.

Other women served as spies, couriers, guides, scouts, saboteurs, smugglers, and informers. Elizabeth Van Lew of Richmond posed as an eccentric known as "Crazy Bet." Under this guise, she rescued Union prisoners from the Richmond prison and operated as a spy. General Grant reportedly said that she was the best spy in his command. Harriet Tubman, the only black person to serve as Union scout and spy, was also known for her great fortitude and cleverness. The Washington society hostess, Rose Greenhow, was said to be very proficient at relaying intelligence to Confederate leaders in code until her house arrest in late 1861 and her dispatch to Richmond. Her efforts reportedly helped the South win the First Battle of Bull Run in July 1861. Belle Boyd also gained prominence as a Confederate spy and courier in Virginia before she was betrayed and arrested in July 1862.

Women were especially effective as couriers and smugglers since hoopskirts, bustles, and false hairpieces could conceal anything from messages to pistols. Both northern and southern soldiers soon overcame their modesty and by late 1861 began searching these good Victorian ladies thoroughly. Louisa Buckner of Virginia was one of the many women arrested after such a search. She had more than one hundred ounces of quinine intended for a Confederate hospital concealed in her skirt. Still, many ingenious women slipped through the lines with goods hidden in false-bottom trunks, parasols, and their crinolines.

Women were also important on the home front during the war years. They kept the farms and plantations going while their menfolk were off fighting. They took jobs in arsenals and munitions factories. They were more visible than ever in mills and other industrial employment. They invaded the offices of the Union and Confederate governments to become clerks who were often called "Government Girls." And they entered the teaching profession by the thousands in both the North and South.

The wartime situation was particularly hard on southern women. In April 1861, when Lincoln's naval blockade cut off the primarily agrarian South from its sources of war supplies, women turned their homes into crude factories to produce what goods they could with limited materials. In addition, they had to deal with the terror of war in their own backyards. They frequently pursued a "scorched earth policy," that is, they burned their own crops and killed their own stock to keep them out of Yankee hands. In 1864, a Virginia woman wrote to her soldier husband: "Chrismus is most here again, and things is worse and worse. . . . Everything me and the children's got is patched. . . . We haven't got nothing in the house to eat but a little bit of meal. I don't want you to stop fighten them Yankees till you kill the last one of them, but try and get off and come home and fix us all up some and then you can go back and fight them a heep harder. . . . We can't none of us hold out much longer down here . . . my dear, if you put off a-comin' 'twon't be no use to come, for we'll all hands of us be out in the garden in the old graveyard with your ma and mine." By the end of the war in April 1865, the want and poverty throughout the Confederacy was incredible.

To stave off the specter of starvation during the latter years of the war, some desperate southern women began pillaging and rioting for bread, especially in New Orleans and Atlanta. Many others supported themselves and their children by taking positions in white schools or by joining the "missionary" teachers flocking in from the North to teach in schools established for freed blacks after the Emancipation Proclamation of January 1863. Others became sewing women or salespeople. Still others took jobs with the Confederate Army that ranged from clerk to engineer. Although many of these women were formerly members of a "genteel elite," wartime conditions and economic need clearly took priority over the standards of White Womanhood that at one time would have prevented them from pursuing some means of sustenance and support.

While the war situation was pushing white women in both the North and South into pursuits that were not consistent with the tenets of either True or White Womanhood, the formal, organized campaign for women's rights had largely disbanded. The last major women's rights convention met in 1861. Many women's rights leaders believed that the abolition of slavery and the end of fighting had to be the center of attention. Others took a more practical approach to the issue. In 1861, suffragist Martha Wright wrote to Susan B. Anthony that it was unwise to argue for women's rights "when the nation's whole heart and soul are engrossed with the momentous crisis and nobody will listen."

When the war ended in April 1865, women leaders who foresaw changes for women as an immediate result of the war met with disappointment. They were dismayed to learn that proponents of abolitionism were much more concerned about the permanent freedom of former slaves than with the status of women. Abolitionist leaders feared that raising women's rights issues in 1865 would complicate, or even prevent, the passage of legislation to protect blacks. Although the Thirteenth Amendment, which abolished slavery was ratified in December 1865, additional protective and civil rights legislation for blacks was under consideration. Its supporters argued that one step should be taken at a time and that women's turn would come eventually. Even black leader Frederick Douglass, who had been sympathetic to women's rights, told them in 1865: "This is the Negro's hour."

When Congress passed the Fourteenth Amendment in 1866, its provisions extended political privileges to white and black men but not to women. The amendment supported the continued disenfranchisement of women by specifically defining citizenship rights as "male," the first time that this word had appeared in the Constitution. Women's rights leaders were outraged. Reformer Frances Gage scathingly wrote: "Can any one tell us why the great advocates of Human Equality . . . forget that when they were a weak party and needed all the womanly strength of the nation to help them on, they always united the words 'without regard to sex, race, or color?' Who ever hears of sex now from any of these champions of freedom!" And Stanton direly predicted, "If that word 'male' be inserted, it will take us a century at least to get it out."

Women's deep concern over their political exclusion erupted at the first major women's rights convention held since the beginning of the war. Meeting in New York City in 1866, delegates unanimously decided that they must push for suffrage for both blacks and women as their primary goals. They duly organized the American Equal Rights Association to work toward these two objectives. In 1866 and 1867, the new organization lobbied and petitioned to have race and gender restrictions deleted from state constitutions. In 1867, the association supported two suffrage bills in Kansas, one for black men and one for women. When abolitionist leaders failed to support the Kansas woman-suffrage bill, the association decided that it was time to part company with their former allies. They became determined to form a new group devoted exclusively to gaining the vote for women.

Suffrage leaders found, however, that many disagreements existed in their own ranks regarding how woman suffrage might best be achieved. As a consequence, two opposing groups emerged. In 1869, Stanton and Anthony formed the National Woman Suffrage Association in Washington. It excluded men from membership and concentrated its efforts on getting Congress to pass an amendment granting women the right to vote. The NWSA published a newspaper coedited by Stanton and Anthony called *The Revolution*. The newspaper's masthead read: "Men, Their Rights and Nothing More, Women, Their Rights and Nothing Less." In addition to working for the immediate enfranchisement of women, the NWSA supported equal pay for equal work, child-care centers for working mothers, and more equitable divorce laws.

Also in 1869, Lucy Stone, Mary Livermore, and Julia Ward Howe, author of the "Battle Hymn of the Republic," organized the American Woman Suffrage Association in Boston. Unlike the NWSA, the AWSA encouraged men to join and focused their efforts on gaining woman suffrage state by state. The AWSA published a newspaper called *The Woman's Journal*, designed to counteract the "radicalism" of *The Revolution*.

When these two rival organizations formed in 1869, public opinion on the issue of extended rights for women was difficult to determine. In 1867 and 1868, Kansas woman–suffrage amendments had failed. In 1868, a woman-suffrage amendment introduced in Congress had also floundered. But, in 1869, Wyoming Territory granted women the right to vote, followed in 1870 by Utah Territory. Although these latter actions were encouraging, they did not precipitate a landslide toward woman suffrage. In all likelihood, as historian Gerda Lerner has noted, "All feared that the hand that rocks the cradle might, given suffrage, also rock the boat." Although the NWSA and the AWSA worked energetically for twenty years, woman suffrage would not be achieved during that period.

In the years immediately following the war, several individual women's rights advocates also joined the fray for women suffrage. An articulate and dramatic woman, Victoria Claflin Woodhull, became the nation's first female stockbroker in 1870, ran for President in 1872, and frequently lectured on women's rights. Along with her equally colorful sister, Tennessee Claflin, she attracted a good deal of attention to the suffrage movement, but she also convinced a lot of people that woman suffragists were highly eccentric.

The Quaker Anna Dickinson was also seen by many Americans as something of a "character." During the Civil War, Dickinson lectured eloquently not only on antislavery but on political and military affairs. She shocked people by campaigning on behalf of political candidates in 1863. After the war, dressed now in elegant gowns accented by extravagant jewelry, Dickinson lectured on injustices to women. Known as the "Queen of the Rostrum" to some, Dickinson exhibited the "worst possible taste" in the eyes of others. Yet, in spite of the controversy that continually swirled around them, Woodhull and Dickinson did draw attention to the cause of woman suffrage while demonstrating that women could effectively enter such "male only" areas as finance and politics.

Evidence suggests that a number of southern women were also interested in women's rights during the postwar years. Although they were not generally as outspoken as their northern counterparts, women such as Sarah Ida Fowler Morgan of South Carolina did make public their women's rights stance. Through editorials in the Charleston *News and Courier* during the 1870s, Morgan examined the "woman question" in great detail. Writing under the pseudonym, "Mr. Fowler," Morgan supported employment, singlehood, and equality for women. But instead of focusing on woman suffrage, she believed that the women's movement should be dedicated to economic independence for women.

Many female reformers in the South and the North rejected the idea of woman suffrage entirely. They feared the evils that women's political participation might introduce into American homes and families. When Catharine Beecher and Harriet Beecher Stowe collaborated in the writing of *Principles of Domestic Science* in 1870, they chose not to support woman suffrage for these reasons. Instead, they wrote: "The authors of this volume while they sympathize with every honest effort to relieve the disabilities and sufferings of their sex, are confident that the chief cause of these evils is the fact that the honor and duties of the family state are not duly appreciated, that women are not trained for these duties as men are trained for their trades and professions, and that, as the consequence family labor is poorly done, poorly paid, and regarded as menial and disgraceful." The sisters outlined woman's "profession" as "the care and nursing of the body in the critical periods of infancy and sickness, the training of the human mind in the most impressible period of childhood, the instruction and control of servants, and most of the government and economies of the family state."

The Beecher sisters' traditional portrayal of American women in the late 1860s and 1870s probably reflected many Americans' views of women. Numerous commentators felt that women should return happily to their homes after the war and focus their full attention on their families. Yet, at the same time, many things had begun to subvert the domestic ideal. Women had learned a tremendous variety of new skills as a result of the war. They had, for example, learned to speak in public, to handle finances, and to serve as executive officers of large organizations through such groups as women's aid societies and the Women's Loyal League. In addition, women moved into formerly "male" jobs, where they proved that they could do heavy labor. They became the arbiters, decision makers, and disciplinarians in their families, which now lacked male heads. And they mastered such new technological devices as washing and sewing machines, which not only reduced the amount of time required to maintain their households but helped to elevate the professional status of housekeepers. Although many women returned to their homes as rapidly as possible at the war's end in 1865, they found it difficult to resume passive, submissive roles.

As a consequence of all the wartime adaptations, American society had gradually come to permit, even to encourage, women's increased entry into a wide variety of endeavors during the 1860s and 1870s. One of these was literature, long a stronghold for achievement-oriented women. But now female authors wrote on such previously taboo subjects as politics and war. Mary Abigail Dodge wrote many outspoken essays of opinion and propaganda under her pen name, Gail Hamilton. In "A Call to My Country-Women," written in 1863, she urged women to aid the war effort. Julia Ward Howe employed poetry to arouse her readers' love of country, the most famous of which was her poem "Battle Hymn of the Republic," written in 1861 and set to music in 1862.

Other women served as newspaper correspondents who shared their wartime experiences and observations with thousands of interested readers. One of these was Charlotte Forten, a black teacher in Georgia, who contributed essays on "Life in the Sea Islands" to *Atlantic Monthly* in 1864. Still other women authors were responsible for an outpouring of books, pamphlets, and tracts designed to raise funds or shape public opinion. And yet other women published personal diaries, reminiscences, and novels written during the war years and afterward.

During the 1860s, several "serious" women authors emerged. Emily Dickinson of Amherst, Massachusetts, wrote many of the 1,775 poems that she would produce in her lifetime during this decade. Although she was little known in her own day, Dickinson is now hailed as the first serious American woman poet because her focus was not on domesticity, but on the larger issues of life, death, immortality, and religion. Dickinson was encouraged in her work by another author of the day and a crusader for American Indian rights, Helen Hunt Jackson. A prolific essayist, poet, and novelist in her own right, Jackson later became known for *Ramona: A Story* (1884), a book championing American Indian women.

Another well-known woman writer of the time was Louisa May Alcott, an author of magazine fiction and novels. In *Little Women*, Alcott portrayed Jo, the central character, as a restless, searching feminist. Interested herself in alternative roles for women, Alcott had one of the novel's characters advise her daughter: "Don't shut yourself up in a bandbox because you are a woman, but understand what is going on, and educate yourself to take part in the world's work, for it all affects you and yours."

While these authors were expanding the scope of women's literary undertakings, other women were taking Alcott's advice to educate themselves and to enter paid employment. Women particularly moved into the schoolroom as teachers. In 1860, women teachers accounted for 25 percent of the nation's teachers. By 1880, women would compose 60 percent of the country's teaching force. In 1865, the *New York Times* commented that teaching was a work "to which intelligent women are preeminently adapted" and "a duty in which many more ought to be engaged."

Women teachers were willing to work for low wages and to accept seasonal employment. As men deserted the teaching profession for better paying jobs in industry or to take up western homesteads, women gladly filled the void. This in turn put pressure upon existing colleges to admit women as students and stimulated the founding of normal schools and women colleges to train female teachers. Vassar College in Poughkeepsie, New York, opened its doors to a class of 353 women in 1865. The curriculum included philosophy, Greek, Latin, German, French, English, mathematics, astronomy, physics, chemistry, hygiene, art, and music. Smith College and Wellesley College offered similar programs when they opened in 1875.

In the South a similar trend developed. Many middle- and upperclass women who now felt the need to help to support their families entered the teaching profession. By 1883, Alabama's superintendent of public instruction noted that "members of the most elegant and cultivated families in the State are engaged in teaching." This movement of southern women into the classroom resulted in a demand for teacher-training schools. In 1875, a normal school opened in Nashville with thirteen women in its student body and two women on its faculty. Several fine southern women's colleges were also established during the postwar years, including Agnes Scott, Goucher, Randolph-Macon, and Sophie Newcomb.

Women also eagerly enrolled in land-grant colleges, which had been coeducational since their underwriting by the Morrill Act in 1862. The presence of female students often created confusion at such schools as Iowa State College, which tried to integrate them into a male-oriented curriculum. Iowa State decided to treat all students as equally as possible, a policy that resulted in uniformed women toting rifles and drilling in military science programs.

Changes in women's sports accompanied these educational developments for women. Vassar College provided facilities for gymnastics, bowling, horseback riding, swimming, skating, and gardening. In 1866, several Vassar women formed a baseball club that played every Saturday afternoon. One young woman commented that "the public so far as it knew of our playing was shocked." Croquet was a much more acceptable game for women and provided the first sport in which women and men could participate together.

There were many other fashionable activities for women. Ice and roller skating were favorites. Bowling became popular, and in 1868, *The New York Clipper* told of a woman who had bowled a 290- and a 300-point game in the same evening. In 1874, Mary E. Outerbridge of New York introduced tennis into the United States. Hampered by long skirts, corsets, and large hats, women played tennis with ladylike grace but little agility. Also in the mid-1870s, archery tournaments, probably the first organized sport for women, became very popular.

In the years following the Civil War, there were many other ways for American women to get into good physical shape. Hundreds of handbooks on diet, appearance, hygiene, digestion, and female health rolled off the presses in an attempt to convince wan, corseted women to begin some kind of physical self-help program. One type suggested mechanical aids such as nose pinchers, shoulder braces, and massage rollers. Others were cosmetic or medicinal in nature and promised both beauty and health. Of these, Lydia E. Pinkham's Vegetable Compound, produced by a family business founded in 1875, became the most famous. In addition, intellectual exercises such as hobbies, reading, and "character development" were recommended.

While women were generally interested in improving their health, many were deeply determined to gain control over their own bodies, especially in the matter of reproduction. Evidence indicates that birth control by abortion had increased during the war years; apparently, women wanted to control their childbearing. This desire to limit family size alarmed many people who felt that it was woman's role to bear many children, feared the possible physical complications of abortion, or believed that the population of the United States would be depleted. In fact, as early as 1829, many states had begun to pass legislation restricting abortions. And in 1832, when Charles Knowlton, a Massachusetts doctor, advocated "checks to conception," he was arrested and fined. This did not deter others from continuing to advertise "Female Monthly Regulating Pills," which were supposedly abortants guaranteed to cure "all cases of suppression, irregularity, or stoppage of the mensus." Newspapers also advertised "Preventive Powders" at five dollars a package and a rubber diaphragm called a "Family Regulator, or Wife's Protector," also costing five dollars.

By the 1850s, medical practitioners and concerned citizens were beginning to be alarmed by the low national birthrate. Accordingly, they accelerated their opposition to planned parenthood and birth control. In 1862, an Ohio obstetrician introduced the first statute banning contraception and abortion. By 1865, many people were more worried about the huge loss of population during the Civil War. The American Medical Association thus launched a full-scale campaign against birth control and abortion. In 1873, these events culminated in the Comstock Law which made it a federal crime to send obscene materials, including birth-control information, through the mail.

Although many women continued to bear unwanted children during the 1860s and 1870s to avoid harm from illegal abortions and to escape legal prosecution, thousands of others continued to seek abortions and birth-control information despite the laws. They were encouraged by such feminists as Elizabeth Cady Stanton, who argued that women were entitled to choose how many children they would bear, and by an industrial, urban economy that made the rearing of large numbers of children more expensive and difficult than it had been on farms. Although technology had not yet offered dependable birth control devices, it had created the conditions that helped motivate women to search for them.

Naturally, technology affected women in many other ways as well. For instance, the emergence of the women's dress-pattern industry during the 1860s democratized female fashions. The mass production of paper patterns enabled women to make their own stylish clothes at will. Before the war, the treadle-powered sewing machine had eased the burden of clothing their families, but had not convinced women that they could devise their own complicated outfits. But then the Civil War stimulated industry, including pattern production. Ebenezer Butterick began his pattern business in 1867 with 12 workers, a number that jumped to 140 in 1870. The availability of paper patterns made fashion at least theoretically accessible to women of every social class and occupation by the early 1870s.

Technology also offered women such new contrivances for the home as improved lamps and stoves. The mystique of domesticity slowed down the adoption of home technology during the 1860s and 1870s because it preached that only unfeminine, lazy, or incompetent women would use new-fangled machines to care for their families. Maintaining an old-fashioned household was such a matter of pride that many women hesitated to accept the aid of mechanical instruments.

Catharine Beecher was the first reformer to call for the adoption of technology, particularly in the kitchen, where, according to her, women spent over 50 percent of their time. In 1869, Beecher designed a model kitchen based on a ship's galley. It incorporated built-in flour and grain bins, a built-in dish draining board, a cast-iron stove set in an alcove with glass doors to block off the heat, and an indoor sink with two pumps, one for rain water and one for well water.

Other women besides Beecher were interested in technology and its applications. Before the Civil War, fifty-five patents were granted to women, but between 1860 and 1888 nearly 3,000 women applied for patents. It is believed that many other women's inventions were patented under men's names. Butterick, for example, is believed to have derived the concept of paper patterns from those created by his wife.

Widespread prejudice and discrimination deterred many women from entering technological and scientific fields and from admitting to any interest in such matters. In 1850, America's first female astronomer,

Maria Mitchell, had been elected to the American Academy of Arts and Sciences for her discovery of the comet that received her name, but another woman was not so honored until 1943. A mid-nineteenth century editor remarked: "If an unfortunate female should happen to possess a lurking fondness for any special scientific pursuit she is careful (if of any social position) to hide it as she would some deformity."

In spite of such discouraging attitudes, women attracted to science continued to pursue their interests. A number of women began to form scientific study groups during the mid-1860s. Groups of women interested in educational reform promoted the introduction of more scientific courses into women's curricula. And, in the 1870s, women approached male scientific societies requesting membership. They were, however, granted only the status of corresponding members who were neither expected to attend the meetings nor allowed to vote.

The practice of law was also difficult for women during the 1860s and 1870s. State licensing bodies simply barred women from taking the required examinations. In 1869, however, Arabella Babb Mansfield applied for admission to the bar in Iowa. She was allowed to take the examinations at the order of a judge who was sympathetic to women's rights. One of her examiners noted that Mansfield passed with high honors, giving "the very best rebuke possible to the imputation that ladies cannot qualify for the practice of law." Mansfield never practiced law, choosing instead to teach at Iowa Wesleyan and later at DePaul University in Indiana.

In the same year that Mansfield became the first licensed woman lawyer in the United States, Myra Bradwell applied to the Illinois Supreme Court for a law license. Bradwell had studied law with her husband while founding and editing the very successful *Chicago Legal News*. An avowed suffragist, she had also drafted several bills to expand women's property rights. In 1869, Bradwell took the licensing examination and passed it with credit, but was denied a license because she was a woman. She appealed her case to the United States Supreme Court, which tossed the matter back to the State of Illinois. Bradwell was finally granted a license in 1890, four years before her death.

Other women soon became "firsts" in the legal field. In 1871, Phoebe Couzins became the first woman to receive a formal law degree when she graduated from Washington University in St. Louis. She was licensed in Missouri but never practiced law. Instead, she became a leading figure in the national woman suffrage movement. A year after Couzins' graduation, Charlotte E. Ray graduated from the law department of Howard University and was admitted to the District bar. She was the first black woman lawyer in the United States and the first woman admitted to practice in the District of Columbia.

Art was another area that attracted talented and ambitious women.

Of course, women continued to produce a tremendous amount of folk art in their homes. Quilts especially reflected current events through the use of such designs as Sherman's March, the Underground Railroad, and the Slave Chain. But when the woman's pavilion at the Centennial Exposition in Philadelphia displayed women's art work in 1876, almost none of the folk art created by self-taught women artists was included. Neither women's folk art nor, for that matter, very much of women's fine art was accorded serious attention or appraisal at that time. In fact, although women had been instrumental in raising the funds for the Centennial Exposition of 1876, they were denied exhibit space in the main exhibition hall and even had to raise additional money for the woman's pavilion.

Women who wanted to practice the fine arts did receive limited encouragement after the Civil War. It was now acceptable for them to move to cities and other countries for art training and to relocate frequently in search of commissions. Still, over half of mid-nineteenth century women artists chose to remain single rather than attempt to combine their demanding careers with marriage. Another change was the gradual admission of women to life drawing classes with nude models, which put them on a more even footing with men in artistic training. And in 1874, when the Art Students' League was established in New York City, it routinely admitted women. At the same time, art was increasingly being perceived as "feminine." In 1860, *The Canyon* claimed that the arts were in harmony with women's delicate and sensitive natures. The arts themselves were seen as embellishment and refinement, so it was not difficult for Americans to begin to think of them as a part of woman's sphere.

During the 1860s, a number of women sculptors emerged. The most prominent of these was Harriet Hosmer of Watertown, Massachusetts. Hosmer had studied in Rome with respected sculptor John Gibson during the 1850s. During the 1860s, her commissions ranged from London to San Francisco. As a sculptor of international repute, Hosmer enjoyed a rich social life, yet declined to marry. At the age of twenty-four, she had written to a friend: "Even if so inclined, an artist has no business to marry. For a man, it may be well enough, but not for a woman, on whose matrimonial duties and cares weigh more heavily, it is a moral wrong, I think, for she must either neglect her profession or her family, becoming neither a good wife and mother nor a good artist. My ambition is to become the latter, so I wage eternal feud with the consolidating knot." Never an ardent feminist, Hosmer did maintain that "every woman should have the opportunity of cultivating her talents to the fullest extent, for they were not given her for nothing."

Hosmer encouraged the work of Edmonia Lewis, a New Yorker of black and Chippewa Indian parentage. Lewis studied briefly with a Boston sculptor in the early 1860s and then went to study in Rome in 1865.

By the 1870s, Lewis had a solid reputation in both the United States and Europe. Her works enjoyed quite a success at the Centennial Exposition of 1876 and demonstrated to many Americans that the artistic production of women could be both interesting and creative.

In the field of music, women composers were also illustrating that, despite such obstacles as lack of opportunities for training, prejudice against publishing their compositions, and the social and economic need to marry, they could produce fine work. By the time of the Civil War, several women composers had achieved public acclaim. Jane Slocum, for example, a young pianist from England, published songs and solo piano compositions into the 1850s. During the 1860s, Faustina Hassae Hodges, daughter of organist Edward Hodges and an organist herself, composed ballads, sacred songs, and piano pieces. One of her songs, "Rose Bush," reportedly sold 100,000 copies. Few American female composers of symphonies and concertos have been identified, but neither were there many American male composers since classical music in America concentrated on European repertory well into the late nineteenth century.

By the 1860s and 1870s, women were not only moving into the arts and professions but into all types of paid employment. Women continued to dominate the needle trades but were now present in growing numbers in retail sales, office work, cigar making, typography, commercial laundries, and various types of mills. Many of the jobs that women filled were "new," that is, they had not previously been filled by men but were created by the growing economy.

Whenever women were hired, wages fell. This was in harmony with the idea that, because woman's place was in the home, she was just an occasional worker interested in "pin money." Actually, numerous women worked to help support their families because many men were disabled or killed during the Civil War or were not paid a living wage. Furthermore, the number of single women who had to support themselves was rising. Yet American employers were still thinking of the ideal woman instead of facing the reality of employed women.

Female workers did not accept the rationalizations offered to them for their low pay, long hours, and terrible working conditions. A number of female workers, like many male workers, came to believe that some form of labor organization might help to improve their situations. Women often turned to men's labor organizations but soon learned that women were usually not welcome. By 1870, thirty-two unions existed in America, but women were barely represented in them, despite the marked increase in the number of women workers since 1860.

Employed women responded to their exclusion from male unions by forming their own groups. For example, the Lady Cigar Makers of Providence, Rhode Island, was organized in 1864. Although women cigar makers accounted for close to 10 percent of all cigar makers, they were denied membership in the national union. Another woman's union, the Collar Laundry Union of Troy, New York, was also founded in 1864. This group was remarkably successful and raised their wages to a level near that of working men. Middle- and upperclass women who continued to be interested in reform after the war organized other types of groups to help working women. Called working women's protective societies, these associations offered services such as legal aid, medical services, and advice to employed women.

In addition to the cause of working women, American women were interested in many other reform issues. Although the reform crusade had lost some of its impetus during the war years, it had not totally disappeared. During the 1860s and 1870s, American women worked for many reforms, including civil rights, woman suffrage, and temperance.

This last reform movement particularly attracted thousands of female supporters. Out of local bands of women who either prayed or destroyed stocks of whiskey came the National Woman's Christian Temperance Union, founded in 1874, with Annie Turner Wittenmyer of Iowa as its first president. To Wittenmyer, the crusade was a fulfillment of woman's moral role in the salvation of humankind. In an address in 1877 Wittenmyer stated her position: "We have been called by the Spirit of the Lord to lead the women of the world in a great and difficult reform movement, and thousands in our own, and other lands, are looking to us with hope and expectation. The drink system is the common enemy of women the world over, and the plans we inaugurate, will be eagerly sought after by the women of all civilized nations, and as the success of all moral reforms depends largely upon women, the world will halt, or move in its onward march toward millennial glory, as we halt or march." This organization soon became the largest woman's organization in the nineteenth century.

Women interested in improving American society also continued their interest in helping the black people of America after the war's end in 1865. Many women participated in the effort to aid newly freed slaves by working for the Freedmen's Bureau, in charity organizations, and as missionary teachers in the South. One of the advocates of relief work for freed blacks was Josephine Griffing, who served as the general agent for the Freedman's Relief Association in Washington between 1865 and 1872. This benevolent organization differed from the government-supported Freedmen's Bureau in many ways. The most notable was Griffing's idea that freed blacks ought to be settled throughout northern and western states at governmental expense. She lobbied Congress to accept her plans while she turned her office and home into a settlement house for freed blacks. Griffing's plan, however, helped no more than a few thousand blacks to resettle.

Black women also worked energetically on behalf of black Americans. Fanny Jackson Coppin, born a slave in the District of Columbia, became an outstanding educator of black youth in the 1870s. Because the southern states seldom made any significant provisions for the education of freed slaves, many educated black women moved south as missionary teachers for black charity schools. Typically, they taught children during the day, adults at night, and held Sabbath schools on Sundays.

Missionary teachers were often supported by missionary and other similar societies dedicated to helping black Americans. In 1864, Sara G. Stanley asked for the support of the American Missionary Association so that she could teach in the South. "No thought of suffering, and privation, nor even death, should deter me from making every effort possible, for the moral and intellectual elevation of these degraded people," she asserted. She would receive ten dollars a month plus board for her efforts.

For black women in the South, the Civil War radically changed their lives in some ways, but not in others. Marriage was now a legal institution for blacks. This resulted in a widespread move to formalize individual marriages and establish stable families including both parents. Massive marriage ceremonies involved as many as sixty or seventy couples. Former slaves worked diligently to locate spouses or children who had been sold away from them, some traveling from state to state and advertising in newspapers.

Marriage and the family might have been recognized legally, but the economic insecurity of the black family remained. Consequently, a large number of newly freed black women labored in the fields or foundries next to men in order to supplement their families' inadequate incomes. Black men who viewed women's labor outside the home as a badge of slavery watched their wives work in the fields and as domestics. Because sharecropping replaced slavery as the dominant mode of production in the postwar South, black women, despite their desire to escape field work, continued to labor in the cotton, tobacco, and rice fields. Other black women took domestic employment as washwomen, domestics, nursemaids, and seamstresses, jobs they had performed as slaves. By 1877, half of adult black women held jobs, while others worked in the fields with their sharecropper husbands.

Freedom offered some advantages to black women workers. Many could now define their own working hours to some extent or could change employers at the end of a contract term. They could marry and bear children without fearing the loss of family members through sale. They also had the opportunity to appeal to authority when dissatisfied. Formal complaints to agents of the Freedmen's Bureau indicated problems that were nevertheless different from those that arose under slavery.

Employers commonly withheld pay to control black women workers and sometimes reacted to them with violence, yet the legal hold of slavery was gone. Women resisted, filed complaints, moved to other plantations, or took other jobs. Wages were low and conditions were difficult, but black women were no longer chattels.

The lives of black women, however, were still circumscribed in many ways. Free black women were denied vocational training and the right to hold certain jobs. While black men were given the right to vote and to hold office in the late 1860s, black women were overlooked. Black men could now own land, but black women seldom had the means to do so.

A large number of rural black women tried to improve their lot by migrating to southern cities. Here they found poor housing, limited job openings, and low wages. In Jackson, Mississippi, and Galveston, Texas, black washwomen protested and went on strike to receive $1.50 per day. Whites arrested the leaders and threatened to require license fees of washwomen. Domestic servants were even worse off. They worked long hours, seven days a week, for which they received low pay supplemented by cast-off clothing and leftover food. Some urban black women tried to escape these evils by selling such goods as spruce beer, peanuts, blueberries, strawberries, and vegetables in local markets. Those women who could raise the necessary capital opened restaurants, grocery stores, and boardinghouses. Despite independence, these urban black women found that their lives were still harsh.

Those black women who migrated to northern cities after the Civil War did not find the opportunities that they had hoped for, either. Like their southern counterparts, they were limited to domestic, menial, and service jobs with long hours and poor pay. In 1871, a northern black woman complained in the Philadelphia *Post:* "Why is it that when respectable women answer an advertisement for a dressmaker, they are invariably refused, or offered a place to cook or scrub, or to do housework: and when application is made to manufactories immediately after having seen an advertisement for operators or finishers, meet with the same reply." These women were further dismayed to learn that, although they paid taxes, their children were denied admission to tax-supported schools because of their race.

Black women, disillusioned with the southern plantation or the urban areas of the South and North, sometimes turned their faces westward during the late 1860s and 1870s. As pioneers and Exodusters (communities of black immigrants, especially in Kansas) they soon discovered that they could not escape racial prejudice. It followed them even into the most progressive of western communities. Once again they were relegated to farm labor and domestic service. In one Iowa town, a black woman who worked as a washwoman for many of the community's white women lived by herself in poverty despite continuous labor and was patronizingly called "Nigger Ellen" by the townspeople. It must have been a harsh blow to learn that even the supposedly egalitarian frontier placed severe limits on the lives of black women.

Southern white women also faced difficult conditions after the Civil War. High-born ladies now learned to perform domestic tasks without the help of servants and to run plantations without the aid of their men who had been disabled or killed during the war. Southern women of all classes were forced to take jobs as clerks, teachers, and industrial laborers to help support their families. The thousands who could not find employment had to depend on rations from northern-based charity groups. Already bitter over the war's destruction of their lifestyles, southern women lived in fear of the black occupation patrols posted in their towns or regions. And when black males were given the right to vote in 1866, many disenfranchised white females were outraged.

Because the labor and any cash income that they produced were now in demand to help keep agricultural enterprises afloat, southern women did seem to gain more respect as farmers after the war. As they moved into the fields and various aspects of farm operations, women proved themselves as workers and managers. One notable female farmer was Frances Butler, the daughter of Frances Kemble and Pierce Butler. When her father died shortly after the war, Butler took over the management of his rice and cotton fields on the sea islands of Georgia. She negotiated labor contracts with black workers, acted as her own overseer, and paid wages without resorting to sharecropping. Many novelists found inspiration in these women. For example, Elizabeth Pringle, writing under the pseudonym, Patience Pennington, dramatized women planters in *A Woman Rice Planter* in 1913.

Western women also participated more fully in farming and homesteading after the Civil War. On the Great Plains, women often managed an isolated claim by themselves while their husbands worked elsewhere to raise the necessary capital for seeds, equipment, and building materials. Others worked alongside their fathers or husbands in "breaking" the claim for cultivation. During the 1870s, one Dakota woman graphically described the demands placed on women settlers: "I had lived on a homestead long enough to learn some fundamental things: that while a woman had more independence here than in any other part of the world, she was expected to contribute as much as a man—not in the same way, it is true, but to the same degree: that people who fought the frontier had to be prepared to meet any emergency: that the person who wasn't willing to try anything once wasn't equipped to be a settler."

Single women also took advantage of the Homestead Act of 1862, which offered a settler a free quarter section of land on the condition that she or he cultivate it for a period of five years. A sample of land office data for Colorado and Wyoming shows that the number of female homestead entrants ranged from 11.9 to 18.2 percent of the total. The data further indicate that 42.4 percent of women succeeded in placing a final claim on their homestead as opposed to only 37 percent of successful men. Frequently called "girl homesteaders," these women were judged an "interesting segment of the population" by one Dakotan.

Since the opening of the Oregon trail and the discovery of gold in California in the late 1840s, female migrants had entered the mining, lumbering, farming, and ranching areas of the far West. They traveled overland, across the Isthmus of Panama, or "around the horn" of South America. In many cases, women found the hardships of the trip less severe than they had feared. Female migrants traded with American Indians, who often were not as fierce and savage as women had been led to believe. As one woman settler later wrote: "We suffered vastly more from fear of the Indians before starting than we did on the plains." Other women raved about the beauty of the prairies, plains, and mountains, and extolled the "wonders of travel." In other cases, however, women became discouraged, frightened, and determined to return to their former homes as soon as possible.

White plains and far western women had lifestyles similar to earlier frontierswomen on agrarian frontiers. An army wife of the 1860s enjoyed her rough and erratic life in frontier forts. She traveled about Kansas and Oklahoma in an army ambulance without much discomfort or danger from Indians. She basked in the attention paid her as one of the few women in camp and decided that "there is considerable romance in my manner of living." Some women, however, found themselves thrust into unexpected situations. In 1874, an Arizona army wife wrote: "I concluded that my New England bringing up had been too serious, and wondered if I had made a dreadful mistake following my husband to Arizona. I debated the question with myself from all sides, and decided then and there that young army wives should stay at home with their mothers and fathers, and not go into such wild and uncouth places."

Other western women with unusual lifestyles were those who took jobs in service industries, including dance halls, saloons, and brothels. Many "soiled doves" who provided companionship and sexual services were hardworking laborers and business entrepreneurs. Irish immigrant Mary Josephine Welch, for example, settled in Helena, Montana, in 1867, where she established the Red Light Saloon. Soon known as "Chicago Joe" after her last hometown, Welch brought in women as dollar-a-dance workers in her saloon. These women, known as "hurdy-gurdy girls" after the popular stringed instrument of the day, earned up to fifty dollars an evening. In 1873, however, Montana passed legislation against dance halls in an attempt to attract a stable family population.

Apparently, women's adaptation depended to a great extent on their backgrounds, personalities, philosophies, and occupations. By the 1860s and 1870s, there were certainly all types of women living in the West. Many were town dwellers who lived in the western settlements that composed the urban frontier. Others were single women in search of employment, husbands, or both. Others were prostitutes who worked the cattle towns and gold camps. Some, like the popular trail guide, Mountain Charley, donned male clothing and assumed male roles. Many were immigrants from Canada, Mexico, Germany, Holland, England, Ireland, Sweden, Norway, and the Orient. Many others were associated with such religious groups as the Church of Jesus Christ of Latter-day Saints, or Mormons, in Utah or the Presentation Sisters in the Dakotas. Others were ardent suffragists, like Abigail Scott Duniway of Oregon. And still others were black, like Mary Ellen "Mammy" Pleasant, a California pioneer and boardinghouse keeper in San Francisco.

Frontierswomen were not only a diverse group but often a politically privileged one as well. The right of suffrage was first granted to women by four western governments. In 1869, Wyoming Territory gave women the right to vote. Supposedly, this occurred because of the urging of Esther Morris and others, who argued that woman suffrage would attract women to Wyoming, thus balancing the population ratio of six men to one woman and introducing a "law and order" faction into rather unbridled Wyoming society. Utah followed with its own woman suffrage law in 1870. Some scholars believe that leaders of the Church of Latter-day Saints wished to insure their political power over the inroads of male non-Mormons, or Gentiles, entering the area. There is some evidence that church leaders were also interested in allowing Mormon women to vote in favor of polygamy, the extremely controversial institution of plural marriage practiced by Mormons at that time.

Largely because of the efforts of Oregonian Abigail Scott Duniway and her suffrage newspaper, *The New Northwest,* Washington Territory passed a woman suffrage measure in 1883, and Idaho in 1896. Although women were thus granted a degree of political participation in these frontier regions, there is little evidence that a revolution in sex roles or women's rights was under way.

Many changes also occurred in the American West for native women. By the 1860s and 1870s, American Indian communities had been disrupted by white settlement, their families torn apart by wars, and the status of women reduced because of the adoption of male-oriented white values. They were increasingly confined to reservations, where their numbers were decimated by malnutrition, famine, and disease. And their children attended reservation schools that attempted to change Indians into pseudowhites by erasing both their culture and their pride in it.

Still, American Indian women of the Plains and other interior tribes did have a measure of choice and control over their lives. White observers often thought that native women were degraded because they performed all domestic and agricultural labor while men engaged in hunting and warfare. Actually, this division of labor extended respect and the right of decision-making to both women and men. Also, Indian women had a degree of control over childbearing. In addition, most Indian cultures stressed the need for both partners to be satisfied in a marriage relationship. Divorce was usually fairly simple to obtain; thus native women could escape abusive, lazy, or intemperate mates without losing their children and personal property as white women usually did.

Furthermore, some American Indian women still exercised a degree of power within their tribes. Occasionally, Plains Indian women served as shamans, medicine people, and warriors. Matrilineal tribes, such as the Mandans of the Dakotas and Tlingits of the Pacific Northwest, vested land in the eldest female of the family who then passed ownership of lands, fields, gardens, houses, and stock through her female descendants. American Indian women also frequently functioned as decision makers and often sat on the council of elders. They participated in decisions that concerned both wars and hunts.

Some Indian women served as spokespeople for their communities by carrying Indian grievances and misgivings to white authorities. The best known of these was Sarah Winnemucca, a Paiute woman from Nevada. In the 1870s and 1880s, Winnemucca served as chief of her tribe and made many futile attempts to save her people from the ravages of white invasion. As a public lecturer dressed in beautiful native garb and the author of *Life Among the Paiutes: Their Wrongs and Claims* (1883), she alerted the nation to the cause of the decimated American Indians.

Winnemucca was far from alone on the lecture circuit during these years. By 1877, when President Rutherford B. Hayes issued the order that removed the army of occupation from the South and technically brought Reconstruction to a close, women were clamoring for all manner of modifications in American society. Women's rights, woman suffrage, civil rights, black rights, temperance, and American Indian rights were some of the issues. Other women who did not mount the lecture platform were also initiating modifications in the prevailing social system by pushing into jobs, professions, and other endeavors previously dominated by men.

Clearly a constant theme during the 1860s and 1870s was women's demand for change. Spurred on by the catalyst of the war and the social upheaval that followed it, thousands of American women made it clear that they did not consider the model of True Womanhood applicable to them. In large, noisy ways or in small, quiet ways, they demonstrated their independence of thought and action. Despite the fact that many Americans still paid homage to the image of the ideal woman, by 1877, ferment and change were definitely beginning to threaten its strength and endurance.

SUGGESTIONS FOR FURTHER READING

Andrews, William D., and Deborah C. Andrews. "Technology and the House-wife in Nineteenth-Century America." *Women's Studies* (1974): 309–328.

Aron, Cindy S. "'To Barter Their Souls for Gold': Female Clerks in Federal Government Offices, 1862–1890." *Journal of American History* 67 (March 1981): 835–853.

Banner, Lois W. *Elizabeth Cady Stanton: A Radical for Woman's Rights.* Boston: Little, Brown and Company, 1980.

Beezley, William H., and Joseph P. Hobbs. "'Nice Girls Don't Sweat': Women in American Sport." *Journal of Popular Culture* 16 (Spring 1983): 42–53.

Berkeley, Kathleen C. "'The Ladies Want to Bring About Reform in the Public Schools': Public Education and Women's Rights in the Post–Civil War South." *History of Education Quarterly* 24 (Spring 1984): 45–58.

Berkin, Carol Ruth, and Mary Beth Norton, eds. *Women of America: A History.* Boston: Houghton Mifflin Company, 1979. Part III.

Blocker, Jr., Jack S., ed. "Annie Wittenmyer and the Women's Crusade." *Ohio History* 88 (Autumn 1979): 419–422.

Brown, Minnie Miller. "Black Women in American Agriculture." *Agricultural History* 50 (January 1976): 202–212.

Brumgardt, John R., ed. *Civil War Nurse: The Diary and Letters of Hannah Ropes.* Knoxville: The University of Tennessee Press, 1980.

Bulger, Margery A. "American Sportswomen in the 19th Century." *Journal of Popular Culture* 16 (Fall 1982): 1–16.

Carrell, Kimberley W. "The Industrial Revolution Comes to the Home: Kitchen Design Reform and Middle-Class Women." *Journal of American Culture* 2 (Fall 1979): 488–499.

Clark, E. Culpepper. "Sarah Morgan and Francis Dawson: Raising the Woman Question in Reconstruction South Carolina." *South Carolina Historical Magazine* 81 (January 1980): 8–23.

Clinton, Catherine. *The Other Civil War: American Women in the Nineteenth Century.* New York: Hill and Wang, 1984. Chapter 5.

Collier-Thomas, Bettye. "The Impact of Black Women in Education: An Historical Overview." *Journal of Negro Education* 51 (Summer 1982): 173–180.

Cowan, Ruth Schwartz. "From Virginia Dare to Virginia Slims: Women and Technology in American Life." *Technology and Culture* 20 (January 1979): 51–63.

de Graaf, Lawrence. "Race, Sex, and Region: Black Women in the American West, 1850–1920." *Pacific Historical Review* 49 (May 1980): 285–314.

DuBois, Ellen C. *Feminism and Suffrage: The Emergence of an Independent Women's Movement in America, 1848–1869.* Ithaca: Cornell University Press, 1978. 53–78.

Dunfey, Julie. "'Living the Principle' of Plural Marriage: Morman Women, Utopia, and Female Sexuality in the Nineteenth Century." *Feminist Studies* 10 (Fall 1984): 523–536.

Elbert, Sarah. *A Hunger for Home: Louisa May Alcott and Little Women.* Philadelphia: Temple University Press, 1984.

Epstein, Barbara Leslie. *The Politics of Domesticity: Women, Evangelism, and Temperance in Nineteenth-Century America.* Middletown, CT: Wesleyan University Press, 1981.

Faragher, John Mack. *Women and Men on the Overland Trail.* New Haven: Yale University Press, 1979.

Foster, Lawrence. "Polygamy and the Frontier: Mormon Women in Early Utah." *Utah Historical Quarterly* 50 (Summer 1982): 268–289.

Godfrey, Kenneth W., Audrey M. Godfrey, and Jill Mulvay Derr. *Women's Voices: An Untold History of the Latter-Day Saints, 1830–1900.* Salt Lake City: Deseret Book Company, 1982.

Gordon, Jean. "Early American Women Artists and the Social Context in Which They Worked." *American Quarterly* 30 (Spring 1978): 54–69.

Gordon, Linda. "The Long Struggle for Reproductive Rights." *Radical America* 15 (Spring 1981): 74–88.

————. "Voluntary Motherhood: The Beginnings of the Birth-Control Movement." In *Family Life in America, 1620–2000,* edited by Mel Albin and Dominick Cavaloo, 131–147. New York: Revisionary Press, 1981.

James, Edward T., ed. *Notable American Women 1607–1950: A Biographical Dictionary.* Cambridge, MA: Belknap Press, 1971.

Jeffrey, Julie Roy. *Frontier Women: The Trans-Mississippi West, 1840–1880.* New York: Hill and Wang, 1979.

Jones, Jacqueline. *Soldiers of Light and Love: Northern Teachers and Georgia Blacks, 1865–1873.* Chapel Hill: University of North Carolina Press, 1980.

Kerber, Linda K., and Jane DeHart Mathews, eds. *Women's America: Refocusing the Past.* New York: Oxford University Press, 1982. Part IIb.

Hedges, Elaine. "The Nineteenth-Century Diarist and Her Quilts." *Feminist Studies* 8 (Summer 1982): 293–308.

Harris, Barbara J. *Beyond Her Sphere: Women and the Professions in American History.* Westport, CT: Greenwood Press, 1978.

Lerner, Gerda, ed. *Black Women in White America: A Documentary History* New York: Random House, 1973.

Lupton, Mary Jane. "Ladies Entrance: Women and Bars." *Feminist Studies* 5 (Fall 1979): 571–588.

Massey, Mary Elizabeth. *Bonnet Brigades: American Women and the Civil War.* New York: Alfred A. Knopf, 1966.

Painter, Diann Holland. "The Black Woman in American Society." *Current History* 70 (May 1976): 224–227, 234.

Painter, Nell. *Black Migration to Kansas After Reconstruction.* New York: Alfred A. Knopf, 1977.

Pursell, Carroll. "Women Inventors in America." *Technology and Culture* 22 (July 1981): 545–49.

Richey, Eleanor. "Sagebrush Princess with a Cause: Sarah Winnemucca." *The American West* 12 (November 1975): 30–33, 57–63.

Riley, Glenda. "Farm Women's Role in the Agricultural Development of South Dakota." *South Dakota History* 13 (Spring/Summer 1983): 83–121.

————. *Women and Indians on the Frontier, 1825–1915.* Albuquerque: University of New Mexico Press, 1984.

Rogers, Gayle J. "The Changing Image of the Southern Woman: A Performer on a Pedestal." *Journal of Popular Culture* 16 (Winter 1982): 60–67.

Ryan, Mary P. *Womanhood in America From Colonial Times to the Present.* New York: New Viewpoints, 1979. Chapter 4.

Schlissel, Lillian. *Women's Diaries of the Westward Journey.* New York: Schocken Books, 1982.

Scott, Anne Firor. *The Southern Lady: From Pedestal to Politics, 1830–1930.* Chicago: University of Chicago Press, 1970.

Stage, Sarah. *Female Complaints: Lydia Pinkham and the Business of Women's Medicine.* New York: W. W. Norton & Company, 1979.

Terborg-Penn, Rosalyn. "Teaching the History of Black Women: A Bibliographical Essay." *The History Teacher* 13 (February 1980): 245–250.

Walsh, Margaret. "The Democratization of Fashion: The Emergence of the Women's Dress Pattern Industry." *Journal of American History* 66 (September 1979): 299–313.

Woloch, Nancy. *Women and the American Experience.* New York: Alfred A. Knopf, 1984. Chapters 9–10.

Gradually, women gained some acceptance in roles and activities outside their domestic sphere. This 1845 engraving presents a number of achievement-oriented women, including several popular authors of the period. From Godey's Lady's Book, Philadelphia, Pennsylvania.

The Resiliency of the Model

BETWEEN 1607 and 1877, the model of what an American woman should be changed in many ways, yet its overall configuration stayed much the same. According to the ideal during these years, a "true" woman was a wife and mother. She was domestic, physically weak, and morally strong. She was too virtuous to participate in politics and too maternal to take paid employment. She could exercise, but only moderately. She could read if the subject matter were morally improving. And, of course, she was fair of skin, with rosy cheeks and flowing brown tresses down her back.

Clearly, the model did not fit many American women. Although there is no way to quantify the number of women who did not conform to the ideal, they were probably in the majority. The fact that the employed, professional, reform, suffrage, immigrant, black, and American Indian women did not fit the model or refused to accept its dictates suggests that thousands of American women lived outside the bounds of the prescribed image.

Yet the stereotype was so prevalent that even women who rejected the ideal in their minds often tried to meet at least part of its teachings in their lives. As a result, such women as Anne Bradstreet and Lucretia Mott set the pattern for later generations of "Super Moms" who would try to care for their homes and families in the "proper" way while attempting to pursue their own personal interests as well.

On the other hand, these same women also struck out against this image, which they challenged and eventually modified to some degree. The model of womanhood was not easily altered or destroyed. It was upheld by women who accepted it with the passivity that was supposedly part of their inherent natures. Other women found its dictates attractive and suitable to their own desires and personalities. And many Americans, both women and men, clung to it because they were afraid to alter a social structure that was known and thus comfortable.

A double theme—the model and reality of American women—runs through women's history, making its study both fascinating and frustrating. Examining the prescriptions for women as well as women's protests against them is, however, despite the difficulties involved, a crucial undertaking if we are ever to understand our collective past. The study of the invented and the actual American woman reveals varied aspects of and numerous insights into the historical experiences of both American women and men.

Fortunately for scholars and others who are curious about the historical heritage of Americans, research in the field of women's history is proliferating at an impressive rate. As one can see from the lists of suggested readings, women's history is a vital pursuit that attracts both female and male scholars and involves a wide variety of journals, topics, and perspectives. Such creativity and growth demands notice. Thus, neither the vitality nor the significance of women's history can be overlooked any longer. Although women's history may seem like a relatively recent development to us, it will not seem so to our children.

Index

Abolitionist movement, involvement of
women in, 56–57, 90, 105, 106–112,
115, 125, 126
Abolitionist societies
black women as members of, 78, 111
formation of, 56
Adams, Abigail, 39, 42–44, 50
Adams, John, 39, 42–43, 50, 52
Adams, John Quincy, 43
Adams, Sam, 38
Adultery, in Colonial America, 13, 24. *See
also* Sexuality
Advocate, The, 97
Afric-American Female Intelligence Society,
79
Agnes Scott College, 130
Agricultural work for women. *See also*
Slavery
during Civil War period, 125
in Colonial America, 13–14, 22–23, 27
on the frontier, 27, 53, 82, 139–140
in Reconstruction period, 139
during reform period, 102–103
in Revolutionary period, 53
Alcott, Louisa May, 129
Algonquian women, lives of, 29, 30
Allen, Mrs., serving of, in King Philip's
War, 17
Alsop, George, 14–15
American Anti-Slavery Society, 108
American Association for the Advance-
ment of Science, 93
American Equal Rights Association, 126
American Fur Company, 69–70
American Historical Association, 5
American Medical Association, 131
American Missionary Association, 137
American Monthly Magazine, 113

American Red Cross, 123
American Revolutionary period, women
during, 37–58
American Temperance Society, 95
American Woman Suffrage Association,
127
Anthony, Susan B., 98, 114–115, 125,
126–127
Antinomians, 20–21
Anti-Slavery Conventions of American
Women, 110
Antislavery movement. *See also* Abolition-
ist movement
Anti-tea leagues, women's formation of, 38
*Appeal for that Class of Americans Called
Africans, An* (Child), 107
*Appeal to the Christian Women of the
South* (Grimké), 108
*Appeal to the Women of the Nominally
Free States, An* (Grimké), 108
Archery, 131
Artists, women. *See also* Folk art
during early industrial period, 73
during Reconstruction period, 133–135
during Revolutionary period, 49–50
Art Students' League, 134
Astor, Jacob, 69–70
Astor, Sarah Todd, 69–70
Asylum for the Repentant (Boston), 97
Atlantic Monthly, 129

Bagley, Sarah, 65
Baltimore, Lord, of Maryland, 12
Barton, Clara, 123
Bascom, Ruth Henshaw, 49, 73
Baseball, 130
"Battle Hymn of the Republic," 127
Beard, Mary R. 4, 42

Beecher, Catharine, 75, 92–93, 94, 128, 132
Beecher, Mary, 92
Belknap, Kitturah, 81
Benevolent organizations. See Charity organizations; Voluntary organizations
Bennett, James Gordon, 112
Berkshire Conferences on the history of women, 5
Bett, Mum, 56
Bickerdyke, Mary Ann, 122
Billings, Phoebe, 26
Birth control. See also Childbearing
  during early industrial period, 72
  during Reconstruction period, 131–132
  during reform period, 100
Blackstone, Sir William, 15
Blackwell, Dr. Elizabeth, 99–100, 122, 124
Blackwell, Emily, 99, 124
Blackwell, Henry, 115
Black women
  in Colonial America, 30–32
  in early industrial period, 76–79
  entrance of, into law field, 133
  entrance of, into medical field, 109
  involvement of, in reform movements, 113, 137
  in Reconstruction period, 137–139
  in reform period, 103–112, 113
  in Revolutionary period, 55–57
Bloomer, Amelia, 96, 112
Boston Female Antislavery Society, 107
Boston Female Moral Reform Society, 97
Boston Seaman's Aid Society, 98
Boston Tea Party, involvement of women in, 38
Bowling, 130–131
Boycotts, women's support of, in Colonial America, 38
Boyd, Belle, 124
Bradford, Gov. William, 13
Bradstreet, Anne, 19, 23, 25, 147
Bradstreet, Simon, 19
Bradwell, Myra, 132–133
Brant, Mary, 29
Brent, Linda, 104
Brent, Margaret, 18
Brook Farm, 97
Brundage, Miss, 73
Bryant, Keith L., Jr., 130
Buckner, Louisa, 124
Bull Run, First Battle of (Civil War), 124
Bulman, Mary, 26
Buras, Anne, 11
Burpee, Sophia, 49
Butler, Frances, 139
Butler, Pierce, 139
Butterick, Ebenezer, 132

Byrd, William, 18–19

Caesarean section, performance of, in Revolutionary period, 48
Calisthenics. See Exercise programs
Calvert, Gov. Leonard, 18
Campbell, Hugh, 31
Canterbury (Conn.) Female Boarding School, 107
Cayon, The, 134
"Captain Molly" (Corbin, Molly), 41
Carey, Mathew, 64
Carlier, Auguste, 74
Cary, Mary Ann Shadd, 110, 113
Centennial Exposition, display of women's art work at, 134, 135
Charity organizations. See also Voluntary organizations
  role of women in, 98, 101, 136
Cherokee women
  during early industrial period, 79
  in early Revolutionary period, 54
Chestnut, Mary Boykin, 105
Chicago Hospital for Women and Children, 124
"Chicago Joe" (Welch, Mary Josephine), 140
Chicago Legal News, 132–133
Childbearing. See also Birth control
  in Colonial America, 11, 25–26
  in early industrial period, 72
  and practice of midwifery, 17, 25–26, 47–48, 78, 98–99
  in Reconstruction period, 131–132
  in reform period, 100
  in Revolutionary period, 47–48
Child, Lydia Maria, 3, 98, 104, 106–107
Chinese women, problems of, in finding jobs in reform period, 102
Christian Science, 97
Civil Death, marriage as state of, 15, 115
Civil War, women during, 121–126
Claflin (Tenn.), 127
Clarke, Amy, 124
Clinton, Catherine, 105
Coffin Quilt, 83
Cohen, Elizabeth, 124
Collar Laundry Union of Troy, New York, 136
Colonial America, women in, 11–32
Commanche women, life of, 80
Commentaries on the Laws of England in 1765 (Blackstone), 15
Commercial enterprises of women
  in Colonial America, 16–18, 22–23
  in early industrial period, 69–70
  on the frontier, 83
  in Revolutionary period, 40

Forest, Anne, 11
Forten, Charlotte, 110, 129
Fort Washington, Battle of (American Revolution), 40
Fourteenth Amendment, 126
Francis, Milly, 80
Freedman's Aid Commission, 110
Freedman's Relief Association, 136
Freedmen's Bureau, 136, 137
Freedom's Journal, 79
Freeman, Elizabeth, 56
Frontier life, for women, 52–53, 80–84, 139–141
Frugal Housewife, The (Child), 107
Fugitive Slave Law, 116
Fuller, Margaret, 114

Gadsden Purchase, 80
Gage, Frances, 126
Garrison, William Lloyd, 107
"Gender specific" experiences, 6
Geneva College, acceptance of Elizabeth Blackwell at, 99
"Girl homesteaders," 140
Goddard, Mary Katherine, 40
Godey, Louis, 89
Godey's Lady's Book, 2, 3, 83, 89–91, 94, 146
Goldsmith, Deborah, 73
Good Wife, God's Gift, A, 19
Goucher College, 130
Government girls, 124–125
Gradual Abolition Law (Pa.), 56
Grant, Gen. Ulysses S., 124
Great Awakening, 26
Greenhow, Rose, 124
Greiger, Emily, 41
Griffing, Josephine, 136
Grimké, Angelina, 108, 109, 110
Grimké, Francis James, 110
Grimké, Sarah, 108, 109, 110
Gymnastics, 130

Hale, Sarah Josepha, 89, 90, 94, 98
Hamilton, Alexander, 64
Hamilton, Gail, 129
Handiwork and crafts. See Folk art
"Handy Betsy the Blacksmith," 40
Harper, Francis Ellen Watkins, 110
Hartford Female Seminary, 92
Hawthorne, Nathaniel, 90
Hayes, Rutherford B., 142
Heebner, Susanna, 49
Hentz, Caroline Lee, 91
Hibbens, Ann, 21
High School for Young Colored Ladies and Misses (Canterbury, Conn.), 107
History, early efforts to reconstruct, 91

History of the Condition of Women (Child), 3
History of the Rise, Progress and Termination of the American Revolution (Warren), 42
Hodges, Edward, 135
Hodges, Faustina Hassae, 135
Hoff-Wilson, Joan, 44, 45
Home for Unprotected Girls (Boston), 97
Home front
women on, in Civil War, 121, 124–125
women on, in Revolutionary War, 39–40
Homestead Act of 1862, 139–140
Hopkins, Anne, 19–20
Horseback riding, for women, 94, 130
Hosmer, Harriet, 134
House of Reception (N.Y.), 97
Howe, Julia Ward, 127, 129
Hunt, Dr. Harriot, 72, 99
"Hurdy-gurdy" girls, 140
Hutchinson, Anne, 20–21, 23
Hutchinson, Thomas, 38
Hutchinson, William, 20

Ice skating, 130
Idaho, women's rights, in 141
Illinois Farmer, 130
Incidents in the Life of a Slave Girl (Child), 104
Indentured servants
arrival of women in colonies as, 12–13
black women as, 31
Indian women
in Colonial America, 27–30
in early industrial period, 79–80
in Reconstruction period, 141–142
in Revolutionary period, 53–55, 57
Industrial expansion, women during, 58, 63–85
Institute for Colored Youth, 110
Iowa Orphans Home Association, organization of, in Dubuque, 122
Iowa State College, 130
Iowa Wesleyan, 133
Irish immigrant women, working conditions for, 102, 140
Iroquois women, in early Revolutionary period, 54
Irvine, Kate, 94

Jackson, Helen Hunt, 129
James, Margaret, 22
Jefferson, Thomas, 38, 52, 56, 57–58
Jemison, Mary, 30
Johnson, Sir William, 29
Journal of a Residence on a Georgian Plantation (Kemble), 114

Moral Motherhood. *See* Republican Motherhood
Morgan, Sarah Ida Fowler, 128
Mormon women, and women's rights movement, 141
Mother's Cathechism and Maternal Instruction, 48
"Mother Society," 101
Motte, Rebecca, 39
Mott, James, 112
Mott, Lucretia, 112, 115, 147
Mountain Charley, 141
Mount Holyoke College, 93
Mr. and Mrs. Woodbridge and Other Tales (Leslie), 91
Murray, Judith Sargent, 50
Musgrove, Mary, 29
Musical achievements of women, 135

Narragansett women, lives of, 29, 30
Nashoba commune (Tenn.), 97
National Anti-Slavery Standard, 107
National Convention of Female Anti-Slavery Societies, 111
National Health Society, 99
National Woman's Christian Temperance Union, 136
National Woman Suffrage Association, 126–127
Native American women. *See* Indian women
New England Antislavery Society, 107
New Northwest, The, 141
New York Central Association of Relief, 121
New York Female Reform Society, 97
New York Infirmary and College for Women, 99
New York Medical College for Women, 124
Norton, Mary Beth, 14, 45
Nurses
  during American Revolution, 40, 41
  during Civil War, 122–123
  in early industrial period, 70

Oberlin College, 98, 115
Observations on the Real Rights of Women (Crocker), 74
"Ode to General Washington" (Wheatley), 41
Oneida, New York, 97–98
Organization of American Historians, 5
Ornaments for the Daughters of Zion, 15
Osborn, Sarah, 26
Outerbridge, Mary E., 131

Paine, Thomas, 38
Panic of 1837, 63, 101
Parke, Mary, 49
Patapsco Female Institute (Baltimore), 93–94
Patent medicine, 99, 131
Pauline doctrine of silence, 21, 75–76
Peale, Charles Wilson, 36, 49
Peale, Sarah Miriam, 49–50
Pember, Phoebe Yates, 123
Pennington, Patience, 139
Pennsylvania Magazine, 41
Pennsylvania Hospital, 47
Perkins, Sarah, 49
Phelps, Almira Lincoln, 93–94
Philadelphia Female Anti-slavery Society, 79, 108, 110
Philipse, Margaret, 17
Pinckney, Charles Cotesworth, 23
Pinckney, Thomas, 23
Pinkham's, Lydia E., Vegetable Compound, 131
Pinney, Eunice, 73
Pitcher, Molly (McCauley, Mary), 40
Place, Sarah Steins, 25
Plains Indian women, lives of, 142
Pleasant, Mary Ellen "Mammy," 141
Pocahontas, 10, 28, 29
Pocasset women, lives of, 30
Powhatan, 28
Powhatan, lives of native women among, 29
Prenuptial agreements, use of, in Colonial America, 16
Presentation Sisters, 141
Principles of Domestic Science (Beecher and Stowe), 128
Pringle, Elizabeth, 139
Proctor, Mrs., 40
Producers Cooperative, 101
Progressives, attack of, on history, 3–4
Property ownership
  during Colonial America, 18
  during Reconstruction period, 133, 139–140
  during reform period, 102, 113
  in Revolutionary period, 45, 49
Prostitution
  during early industrial period, 66
  during reform period, 101, 102
Providence (R.I.) Employment Society, 98
Purvis, Harriet Grimké, 110

Quaiapan, 30
Quakers, 26, 115

Ramona: A Story (Jackson), 129